WAIATA
MAORI SONGS
IN HISTORY

Also by Margaret Orbell

Maori Folktales   1968
Contemporary Maori Writing (ed.)   1970
Traditional Songs of the Maori (with Mervyn McLean)
   1975 (rev. 1990)
Maori Poetry: An Introductory Anthology   1978
The Natural World of the Maori   1985
Hawaiki: A New Approach to Maori Tradition   1985

About the author

Margaret Orbell is a leading authority on traditional Māori literature and mythology. Born in Auckland in 1934, she was editor of the Māori Affairs Department journal *Te Ao Hou* from 1961 to 1965, and later gained her Ph.D. in Anthropology at the University of Auckland with a thesis on waiata aroha. She taught Māori at the University of Auckland (1974-75) then moved to Christchurch, where she is presently Reader in Māori at the University of Canterbury.

She has published numerous books and articles, in New Zealand and elsewhere, on traditional Māori literature and thought.

WAIATA

MAORI SONGS IN HISTORY

an anthology introduced and translated by

MARGARET ORBELL

Overleaf: A meeting of rangatira on the marae at Kaitotehe, an important Waikato village at the foot of Taupiri Mountain.

A RAUPO BOOK
Published by the Penguin Group
Penguin Group (NZ), 67 Apollo Drive, Rosedale,
North Shore 0632, New Zealand (a division of Pearson New Zealand Ltd)
Penguin Group (USA) Inc., 375 Hudson Street,
New York, New York 10014, USA
Penguin Group (Canada), 90 Eglinton Avenue East, Suite 700, Toronto,
Ontario, M4P 2Y3, Canada (a division of Pearson Penguin Canada Inc.)
Penguin Books Ltd, 80 Strand, London, WC2R 0RL, England
Penguin Ireland, 25 St Stephen's Green,
Dublin 2, Ireland (a division of Penguin Books Ltd)
Penguin Group (Australia), 250 Camberwell Road, Camberwell,
Victoria 3124, Australia (a division of Pearson Australia Group Pty Ltd)
Penguin Books India Pvt Ltd, 11, Community Centre,
Panchsheel Park, New Delhi – 110 017, India
Penguin Books (South Africa) (Pty) Ltd, 24 Sturdee Avenue,
Rosebank, Johannesburg 2196, South Africa

Penguin Books Ltd, Registered Offices: 80 Strand, London, WC2R 0RL, England

First published by Reed Publishing (NZ) Ltd 1991
Reprinted 1994, 2000, 2002, 2004, 2005 (twice)
New edition reprinted 2006, 2007

First published by Penguin Group (NZ) 2009
    5 7 9 10 8 6 4

Copyright © Margaret Orbell 1991

The right of Margaret Orbell to be identified as the author of this work in terms of section 96 of the Copyright Act 1994 is hereby asserted.

Printed in China through Bookbuilders, Hong Kong
Designed by Neysa Moss
Typeset by Rennies Illustrations Ltd

All rights reserved. Without limiting the rights under copyright reserved above, no part of this publication may be reproduced, stored in or introduced into a retrieval system, or transmitted, in any form or by any means (electronic, mechanical, photocopying, recording or otherwise), without the prior written permission of both the copyright owner and the above publisher of this book.

ISBN: 978 0 14 301196 5

A catalogue record for this book is available
from the National Library of New Zealand.

www.penguin.co.nz

Acknowledgments

Like all students of waiata, I am greatly indebted to the Māori and Pākehā scholars who for 150 years have recorded, interpreted, studied, preserved and taught Māori poetry and tradition. Most of those whose work I have drawn upon in this instance are listed in the notes and references.

I am most grateful for the assistance I received from the late Riki Ellison and Arapeta Awatere.

For their advice and assistance, I wish to thank Merimeri Penfold, Myra Couch, Te Rangianiwaniwa Rakuraku, Lyndsay Head, Colin Brown, John Hearnshaw and my editor, Jem Bates.

Some of the material in this book appeared first in *Poetry New Zealand, Tu Tangata, Landfall* and *Untold.* Two texts and translations are from *Traditional Songs of the Maori* by Mervyn McLean and Margaret Orbell (Auckland University Press, revised ed. 1990).

Contents

Acknowledgments   *vii*
Introduction   1

1   *Lament for a Rangatira*   7
2   *Te Ika-here-ngutu's Lament for His Children*   11
3   *Love Song*   19
4   *Te Rarawa-i-te-rangi's Protest*   23
5   *The Song about Turner's House*   27
6   *Lament for Tāmati Tara-hawaiki*   31
7   *Te Whare-pōuri's Lament for Nuku-pewapewa*   37
8   *Lament for Te Iwi-ika*   43
9   *Kāhoki's Song for Petera Te Puku-atua*   47
10   *Lament for Ngaro*   51
11   *Mihi-ki-te-kapua's Song for Her Daughter*   55
12   *Tatai's Song for Te Toa-haere*   61
13   *Rangiamoa's Lament for Te Wano*   65
14   *The Exile's Lament*   71
15   *Puhiwāhine's Song about Her Lovers*   77

16 *Football Song* 87

17 *Song for Te Whiti* 91

18 *Lament for Parata* 97

Notes   103
Glossary   111
References 113
Credits   115

Introduction

IN TRADITIONAL Māori society there was a great deal of singing, in everyday situations as well as on special occasions. The choice of song depended upon the circumstances. When there was direct assertion rather than complaint, a song was usually performed in recited style, without melodic organisation. Such recited songs were often associated with vigorous action or a strong social challenge. They included, among many others, paddlers' songs (tuki waka), dance songs (haka), women's vaunting songs in reply to insults (pātere), and watchmen's songs (whakaaraara pā).

There are also three kinds of songs that were mainly concerned with the expression of love and sorrow, and often took the form of a personal communication. These songs were sung rather than recited, with a melody repeated in each line and the language shaped accordingly. The kind known as oriori were usually sung to communicate to a boy or girl the tribal circumstances they had inherited, and the relatives who would offer their support. Those known as pao were epigrammatic couplets, mostly sung for entertainment, which expressed love, extended greetings and commented upon local events and scandals. The third kind, waiata, are those with which this book is concerned.

Waiata were by far the most important of the melodic songs. They were generally laments or complaints and were usually sung publicly, on a marae or elsewhere, to express the poet's feelings, convey a message and sway the listeners' emotions. Their language is often elaborate, with specialised expressions and complex allusions. They were sung very slowly, with melodies in which endlessly inventive use was made of a small range of notes.

There are different kinds of waiata. The greatest poetic energy was devoted to the waiata tangi, literally 'weeping waiata', which were usually laments for the dead (though occasionally a song mourned another loss, such as that of land or crops, or illness). Waiata tangi were composed by both men and women. They were sung at funerals by individuals and by groups of people, and afterwards as well when it was appropriate to remember and mourn the person who had died. In 1817, a Pākehā missionary at Pēwhairangi (the Bay of Islands) was present at a meeting attended by groups of people from the surrounding districts: 'there was a general mourning for two days and two nights', and persons 'continued to rise up alternately during the whole time and sing a mournful song to the memory of their departed relatives. . . . [They] did not cry nor cut themselves, as they usually do when a person is recently dead'.

As well as paying tribute to those who were gone, the singing of laments reinforced the ties that bound the living and provided a link with the past. A song composed for a famous person might be sung without modification at the funerals of his or her descendants, in recognition of their ancestry, or an old lament might be adapted to fit new circumstances. In such ways many waiata tangi passed down through the generations and travelled from one part of the country to another.

Two kinds of waiata were composed only by women. Waiata aroha, 'waiata of love and longing', usually take the form of complaints about unrequited love, gossip concerning the poet, her family's refusal to let her marry the man she wants, or a neglectful husband or lover. The singing of a clever, heartfelt waiata aroha was a highly assertive act. For a woman in difficult domestic circumstances, it might well influence the persons to whom it was addressed and at the very least would improve her social position. And a girl's complaint about a man's indifference was an accepted way of declaring her love and encouraging a response.

Waiata whaiāipo, 'sweetheart waiata', are bolder still. Often the poet would speak of her love for several men, addressing each in turn and sometimes sending herself on an imaginary journey to visit them. These witty, flirtatious songs were sung mostly for entertainment, though they might, in fact, convey messages to some of the men addressed.

Waiata aroha and waiata whaiāipo were sung publicly by the poet, then later by others. They were sung for entertainment (often at night, especially when the moon was full), and they were sometimes sung in memory of the poet or the man she had loved. Or again, a woman might see herself as being in a situation similar to that of the poet, and adapt the words to her own circumstances.

Orators quoted from waiata in their speeches, and had to be familiar with a wide range of songs suitable for different occasions. A rangatira at Matatā welcomes guests at a feast.

But it was not only women who put familiar love songs to their own use. Men did so too, in oratory. If a rangatira, for instance, wanted another leader as a political ally, he might in the course of a speech sing a well-known waiata aroha with the words modified in such a way as to identify himself with the woman poet, and the desired ally with her distant lover. A telling reinterpretation of an old song conveyed a persuasive message to the orator's audience.

The poets' concerns began to change in the early nineteenth century as the people acquired a new technology, new resources, a new religion, then in 1840 a superimposed political structure and a foreign queen. The Treaty of Waitangi brought peace between the tribes, so that there were no more deaths in battle to lament, and biblical stories began to replace some of the old religious traditions. The poets began to speak of their new interests and concerns, and soon of the struggle to maintain their mana and their heritage as the country became overrun with Pākehā

At the end of his speech an orator on the marae will sing an appropriate song, being joined by others. In 1961 at Pūtiki, Whanganui, a visiting Waikato party are saying their farewells. The singers are, from left, Dr Pei Te Hurinui Jones (Ngāti Tūwharetoa and Waikato), Mrs Mona Te Kopa (Waikato), Mrs Rangi Metekingi (of Whanganui and Ngāti Kahungunu) and Dr Henare Tuwhangai (Waikato).

settlers, and in many regions the colonial Government overcame Māori resistance and seized tribal lands. There were songs of protest about Pākehā greed, and songs by, or about, a series of prophetic leaders, notably Tāwhiao, Te Kooti and Te Whiti. Late in the century some waiata were still being composed, along with songs such as haka and pao; in the early years of the twentieth century they became a major influence upon the new styles which evolved, and contemporary Māori poets and composers continue today to draw inspiration from this great poetic heritage. As well, some old waiata are still sung, usually on the marae, by singers and orators who keep alive the ancient tradition.

Sir Apirana Ngata (1874-1950), who with Dr Pei Te Hurinui Jones produced *Nga Moteatea*, an important three-volume collection of waiata and oriori.

Thousands of texts of waiata and other songs, most of them still unedited and untranslated, survive in manuscripts in public libraries and in early books and periodicals. These songs were written down almost entirely by Māori authorities, from the 1840s onwards, and they were then preserved in most cases by interested Pākehā. Since this time Māori and Pākehā scholars have continued to study waiata and other songs, along with traditional narratives and other early writings. The two leading scholars in this century have been Apirana Ngata and Pei Te Hurinui Jones.

The present anthology is intended as an introduction to the waiata of the nineteenth century. So far as possible it follows a chronological sequence, tracing the poets' responses to public and private events. Men and women mourn and praise famous people and those known only to their own relatives, they celebrate Christianity and the hope it brings, they lament defeats then look to the future, and they celebrate the teachings of the leaders whose prophecies sustain them. And throughout these years the women poets assert themselves strongly, as they had always done, in waiata aroha and waiata whaiāipo. These voices from the past continue to convey their experience.

~1~
Lament for a Rangatira

AT A TANGIHANGA, relatives and friends gathered to honour the dead and affirm their ties with the living. It was thought that the wairua, the soul, remained with the body for three days and nights, and during this time the mourners wept and addressed the deceased in oratory and song. They spoke of their grief, they offered praise, they recalled the past, if necessary they promised revenge, and they helped the person to make the transition from this world to the next; as an early Pākehā visitor remarked, the soul was 'sung out of the body'. Sometimes the wairua was believed to mount to the skies, where the left eye might become a star, but usually it was thought to make its way by water to Te Rēinga, the entrance to the underworld in the Far North.

In a song by an unknown poet, a rangatira is sent along peaceful, 'windless' paths.

HARE RA, E PĀ

Hare ra, e pā, i te ara hau-kore.
Taku ate hoki ra, taku pākai riri ki te ao o te tonga,
Taku manu kōrero ki te nohanga pahī,
Taku manu hakahaka ki runga ki ngā iwi!
Houhia mai ra te matua ki te kahu tahu-whenua,
Houhia mai ra te matua ki te kahu taha-ā-rangi.

Marewa, e te iwi, nāna i whītiki!
Taku mōtoi kahurangi ka mau ki te taringa,
Taku koko tangiwai ka mau ki te kakī,
Taku pou mataaho e tū i te whare,
Kia tū mai koe i te ponaihu o te waka,
Kia whakarongo koe te wawara tangi waihoe.
Waiho i muri nei tō pūkai kura ī.

SET OUT, SIR

Set out, sir, along windless paths.
O my heart, my shelter against the southern clouds,
My bird that spoke when the tribes gathered,
My bird that soared above the people!
Clothe our father in the kākā feather cloak,
Clothe our father in the tui feather cloak.
Lift him up, my people — he who girded himself!
My ear pendant of pale greenstone,
My neck pendant of transparent greenstone,
My window-post that stood in the house,
Stand at the prow of the canoe
And listen to the sound of the paddles moving together.
Leave behind here the mourners whom you love.

THE MAN who is mourned is said to have been his people's screen, or shelter, against the enemy (who are identified with the fierce south wind and the clouds it bears). He is likened to a bird because his powerful oratory was as beautiful as the singing of birds, and because as a leader he rose high above his people. The warrior who girded himself for battle must now be clothed in fine garments and carried to his resting place.

In the last lines there is more praise as the rangatira is likened to pendants of the finest greenstone, and a window-post (which as a source of light is symbolic of knowledge). Addressed in these terms, in a passage of high eloquence, he is told he must stand at the bow of the canoe — a place of honour — as it conveys him across the water. The poet may be

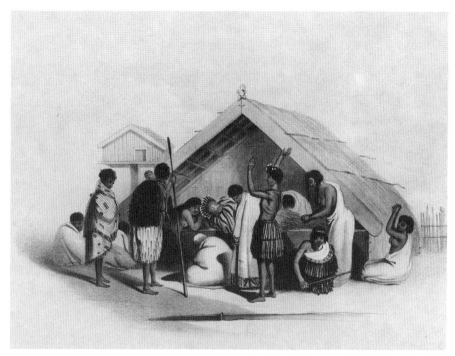

The tangihanga of a rangatira in the early 1840s. He lies in the porch of a house, his head adorned with huia plumes.

speaking of a voyage made in reality to take the body to the tribal burial place, perhaps on a tapu island. But even if this is so, the actual canoe must at the same time be associated with the mythical one which in tradition is often said to take wairua to the underworld. With the proper ceremonies performed, with tears, praise and honour, the rangatira is sent on his last voyage and separated from the kinsmen who mourn him.

2

Te Ika-here-ngutu's Lament for His Children

SOMETIMES an eloquent song passed from one singer to another until it was being sung in regions remote from that in which the poet had lived. This happened when a rangatira of Ngāti Ruanui, in southern Taranaki, composed a waiata tangi mourning the deaths of his children.

Some had been killed in 1822, when their people had been defeated by a large war party, known as Te Āmio-whenua (The Encircling-of-the-land), which had fought its way south from the Tāmaki district armed with muskets — new, terrifying weapons. Others had died as the result of illness. In his song Te Ika-here-ngutu lamented the deaths of all his children, mentioned a son who had just departed, then spoke of these disasters as part of a general cataclysm that had left his people weak and defenceless. Finally he addressed the son whose death had just occurred. Recalling his prowess as a warrior, he wished that he had died gloriously in the fight with the northern invaders.

NEI KA NOHO, KAPAKAPA TŪ ANA

Nei ka noho, kapakapa tū ana
Te tau o taku manawa ki aku tamariki.
Etia nei au, e tama mā,
Ko te Aitanga a Tāne e tuohu'i uta ra —
E piko nei me te mamaku ki aku tamariki.
Kei whea ra, ē, te tamaiti

I karangatia ai, 'Nau mai, e tama.'
Ka riro rāia i te taiheke nui.

Ka noho tēnei au, e tama mā,
I runga i te kāhui papa,
Papa mania, papa tahia, tahia rawatia.
Kei ai he titiro i te rā e tū iho nei,
Te maunga e tū mai ra ki te hau kāinga
I whakaarohatia mai e te kōnohi tonga.
Tēnei me ruru ki te whare na Whiro-te-tupua.
Kei wareware taku ngākau ngā hanga a te rau.
Me i kaiā rānei te marama, i mate ai?
Me i kaiā rānei te pari, i horo ai?
Ngā huri nei, i pirau ai?
Me i taua mea, ka ruru ngā atua ki a tātou,
Ka ngaro i te ngaro a te moa.

Ko te rau kau 'nō te whakawaia ana
Ki te whānau a Pani, a Rongotau,
Nāna te kāhui kura, ngā taonga whakamanamana,
E tama mā, a ō kuia aua atu ko tawhiti.
Nāku pea koutou koi tiki atu
Ki Hawaiki ahu mai ai,
Ka tupu koutou hei tāngata.
Ka rangaa e ō tūpuna ngā hau o te pō,
O te pukupuku, o te tau mate,
Hoki mai 'nō ki te pūkai wheo ai.

I tohia ai koe ki te tohi
O Tū-torohakina, o Tū-te-nganahau,
Kia karo riri tama,
Kia karo nguha, kia karo patu.
Kei te whakahira koe
I te riri kaiapa na ō mātua
Ki roto o Kairau,
Kia ruku atu koe te ruku a te kawau,
Ka ea tō ika, he haku no te moana uri,
Ka kō ō rongo i runga Haumātao.
E uia mai koe e ngā whenua,
'Ko te tama a wai?':

'Ka toa, ka rangona,
Ka tū i te ihu o te waka, ka rangona,
Ka amohia te iwi, ka tiketike ki runga,
Koia Patu Āpiti, te kiri kai-mata.'
Kīhai taku tamaiti i waiho e au
I roto o Ngaengae.
Ki' whakaata koe, ē, Tōtara-i-ahua
Ki te pū whakakeko,
Ki' tere mātoru koutou ko ō mātua ki roto o Manukau,
E kore au e mihi atu ki a koutou.

I SIT HERE WITH MY HEART-STRING

I sit here with my heart-string
Beating and rising because of my children.
Men, I am like the Descendants of Tāne
Bent over in the interior,
I am drooping like the mamaku because of my children.
Oh where is the child
To whom I called, 'Come here, my son'?
He is borne away on a tide ebbing far out.

Men, here I sit
On the sands where the flocks live,
Slippery sands, sands swept bare, everything swept away.
Let me not gaze upon the sun standing above,
The mountain standing over there by our home
For which I long with yearning brought by the south wind.
I must be confined within the house of Whiro-the-demon.
Let my heart not forget the deeds of the multitude.
Was the moon stolen when it died,
Was the cliff stolen when it fell,
These seed kūmara, when they rotted?
If it be so, the spirits have closed upon us
And we are lost, lost like the moa.

Now there are only the leaves, deceiving us,
From the family of Pani and Rongotau

To whom belong the precious clusters, the treasures,
My sons, that gave joy to your mothers
Who are now gone far away.
It was I who fetched you from Hawaiki,
Forming you here, so that you became men.
Your ancestors raised the winds of night,
Of gooseflesh, seasons of death.
Now they come upon us, and we are crouched and groaning.

You were dedicated with the ritual
Of Tū-torohakina and Tū-te-nganahau
So you could defend yourself, my son,
Against hostility, attacks and blows.
You were eager to do battle
In the fierce wars of your fathers
On the Kairau plain,
To dive as a shag dives
And come up with your fish, a kingfish
From the dark-green ocean!
And your fame resounded over Haumātao!
If you are asked in other lands,

A tūtū waewae, a war dance, performed by men holding traditional weapons, hatchets and muskets.

The first tribes to acquire guns and ammunition gained a great military advantage. An early carving depicting the Ngāpuhi rangatira Tāmati Wāka Nene holding a musket.

'Whose son are you?':
'The brave are known,
Those who stand at the prow of the canoe are known,
They are lifted up by their people, raised up above.
So men with patu fight together, naked bodies!'
I did not leave my child at Ngaengae.
If you had been aimed at by Tōtara-i-ahua
With the levelled gun,
And you and your fathers, thronging together,
Had floated to Manukau,
I would not have greeted you with tears.

IN THIS LONG, complex song there is much imagery. In the first lines the mamaku, tallest of the tree ferns, is a descendant of Tāne, who personifies the forest; its immense fronds were traditionally seen as drooping with sorrow. The ebbing tide was also associated with death.

In the second verse, Te Ika-here-ngutu and his people are likened to flocks of sea birds standing on the beach and made homeless by the incoming tide. The poet refuses to gaze upon the sun, for it represents everyday life, while he is the prisoner of Whiro-te-tupua (Whiro-the-demon), the mythical figure who bears men off to death. The 'multitude' who have attacked his family must be the spirits; these were thought to determine whether human beings lived or died. The waning moon and crumbling cliffs represent death and defeat. If the deaths of Te Ika-here-ngutu's children (whom he likens to seed kūmara) are part of a more general disaster brought about by the spirits, he and his people will be utterly destroyed. Such an irretrievable loss would be comparable to that of the moa, the great bird which in most places had been hunted to extinction by the sixteenth century.

In the third verse there is a further development of the image in which kūmara represent human life. Te Ika-here-ngutu recalls the fertility of the past while lamenting its destruction: life appears to continue, but only the leaves of the kūmara are left and there is no substance beneath, for both men and food are gone to the underworld. Pani and Rongotau are mythical figures associated with the origins of the kūmara — here spoken of as 'precious clusters' and 'treasures'. The 'kuia', mothers and aunts, are those who once grew the kūmara and reared the children. Now both kuia and children are gone.

Having spoken of his children's mothers and aunts, Te Ika-here-ngutu turns to his own role as their father. It was believed that every child had its origin in the homeland of Hawaiki, where its genesis repeated the creation of the first person by the mythical Tāne; fathers were thought to take upon themselves, and re-enact, the role of this first male creator. The poet recalls the deeds of valour performed by his ancestors and compares his people's position then with their unhappy situation now.

The last verse is addressed to the son who has just died. Te Ika-here-ngutu recalls the young man's career as a warrior, speaking of the ceremony in which he was dedicated to war when an infant and quoting phrases from the ritual chant recited during this ceremony; Tū-torohakina and Tū-te-nganahau are mythical figures associated with warfare. He speaks of his son's bravery in a battle fought on the Kairau plain, near Waitara, and the fame he won amongst his people on this occasion (Haumātao is a hill in the territory of Ngāti Ruanui, near Hawera). He then praises his son in the guise of telling him how he must answer if he should be challenged as to his identity: 'ngā whenua', other lands, must be those he will pass through on his way to the underworld. Ngaengae must be the place where Ngāti Ruanui had been defeated by the enemy war party Te Āmio-whenua.

In traditional times it was thought that the best way for a warrior to die was in battle, falling before his foes. Te Ika-here-ngutu expresses the wish that, instead of dying as a result of illness, his son had died valiantly in the fight against Te Āmio-whenua. The most glorious death of all would have been to be killed by Tōtara-i-ahua, one of the small number of enemy rangatira who possessed a musket. At this time the extraordinary power of these new weapons gave them great prestige. Some of the young man's 'fathers' (his uncles, and other male relatives of that generation) had died in this battle, and their souls had made their way northwards, past the Manukau Harbour, to the underworld. It would have been better if his son had accompanied them.

If that had happened, the poet claims, there would have been no need for elaborate mourning or the composition of a lament. He would have had the satisfaction of knowing his son had died bravely, and there would have been the prospect, however distant, of his people's eventually taking revenge for his death. While tears and laments provided utu, or com-

Te Wherowhero, the leading rangatira of the Waikato tribes, mourned the death of his younger brother Kati with this song.

pensation, for a man's death, the best compensation was the defeat of an enemy.

Te Ika-here-ngutu's waiata tangi was soon being sung far from his home, sometimes by enemy tribes. Its words made it an especially appropriate lament for old people who had lost a number of younger relatives. In 1853, George Grey remarked that Te Wherowhero, the leading rangatira of the Waikato tribes, had mourned the death of his younger brother Kati with this song, and that it was 'always sung by the aged chiefs if many members of their family die'. In an account by John White there is a description of the manner in which it was sung in the Hokianga district, far to the north. At a funeral, the bodies of two young people who had died were placed in a wharau, a shelter, on the marae.

> The people now gathered round this house of the dead, and those nearest sat down in a circle, about twenty paces from the wharau, while the others remained standing. They sang, as with one voice, a song composed as a dirge. . . .
>
> > How throbs my heart for you, O my children!
> > As droops the palm fern in the forest gloom,
> > So droops my beating heart for you. . . .
>
> This was an old song, and only known to the old people whose voices kept perfect time while singing it. The young people did not join in singing; but at the end of each stanza, they took up the chorus of sobs, while the others rested for a short time, again to take up the wail.

While White tells us that the song was 'only known to the old people', it seems that old people were in any case regarded as the proper persons to sing it. They apparently sang only the first two verses, which lament the young people's deaths in words equally applicable to their own circumstances. Almost certainly they did not know the poet's name or tribe. These were unimportant, and indeed the poet's anonymity may have helped to give his lament a general significance. Singing it, the old people were at one with all the elders who in earlier times had mourned disasters that had befallen their families.

3
Love Song

OFTEN IN A WAIATA whaiāipo, a sweetheart song, a woman would claim to be in love with several men, speaking of each in turn. These were usually light-hearted songs sung mostly for entertainment, though a poet might take the opportunity to speak her mind to someone with whom she had been involved, or encourage a man she particularly liked. Sitting by a famous waterfall on the western shore of Lake Taupō, an unknown poet of Ngāti Tūwharetoa made up a song about three men, Mōhaka, Te Whatu and Hemana.

TŌKU TAUMATA TONU

Tōku taumata tonu te rere ki Waihī,
Mārama te titiro te puia i Tokaanu.
Kai raro Mōhaka — he tau koe na Kiore ī!
Aua, e whae, e nuia ō riri.
Kāore nei hoki au e hihiri atu ana —
Na te ngutu o te rau nāna rawa i hāpai,
Ka rongo Te Kōhika i ōku kōrero.
Nāku i taiapo te maru ra i a Te Whatu,
Ka pono anō ra ko te awhi-ā-kiri.
He mea mahue au te kaunuku haere
I a Tūhourangi ki te tai ki te muri,
Ki taku tūmanako i te raro, i a Hemana!

MY LOOKOUT-PLACE

My lookout-place is always the Waihī waterfall
Where I can see clearly the hot springs at Tokaanu.
Mōhaka is below there — you are Kiore's beloved!
Don't be too angry with me, madam,
I don't want him at all,
It's the lips of the multitude that lift it up
So Te Kōhika hears the stories about me.
Yes I did seize the shelter of Te Whatu,
It's quite true there were embraces.
I was left behind when the Tūhourangi people
Went on their journey to the northern region
And to Hemana, the man down there I want so much!

WOMEN IN LOVE would often sit at a lookout-place from which they could glimpse a hill, or other landmark, near which their man was living; here the poet speaks of sitting by the top of the Waihī waterfall and gazing across the bay at the steam rising from the hot springs at Tokaanu, Mōhaka's home. But then she reminds Mōhaka that he already has a wife, Kiore, and she assures Kiore she has no designs upon him — this story is only gossip, which has spread so far it has reached the village of Te Kōhika. Perhaps she had shown some interest in Mōhaka, but is now saying she is not willing to be his second wife; perhaps there had been groundless gossip; or perhaps nothing at all had happened and she is only teasing Mōhaka and Kiore.

A woman who was the subject of gossip would sometimes save face by boldly admitting the charge and confronting her critics. Having denied an involvement with Mōhaka, the poet admits there has indeed been an affair with Te Whatu. Lastly she speaks of Hemana, who lives apparently in the Lake Tarawera district, the home of Ngāti Tūhourangi. A travelling party from this region had, it seems, visited Taupō; she wishes that she had been able to accompany them on their return and see Hemana there. Very likely he was known to her only by repute, for the composers of waiata whaiāipo often speak in this way of famous rangatira in neighbouring tribes. Hemana's name, mentioned at the end of her song, comes as a climax. She does not want Mōhaka; yes, she has slept with Te Whatu; the man she really wants is Hemana, far away.

The Waihī waterfall near Pukawa, on the western shore of Lake Taupō.

Waiata whaiāipo were sung first by the poet and then by others, often for many years and in parts of the country where the singers knew nothing of the persons and circumstances concerned. Regardless of these, the songs' spirited sentiments, clever expressions and beautiful melodies made them memorable, so that they were sung with enjoyment and passed down in tradition.

4
Te Rarawa-i-te-rangi's Protest

MOST RANGATIRA had several wives, for the maintenance of their mana depended very largely upon these women's skill and industry in the fields, in food-gathering and in weaving. Usually a man chose a high-ranking woman as his wahine matua, main wife, then later took other women as his wāhine iti, little wives. Female slaves might become his wives as well.

Sometimes a woman was glad to have a co-wife to help with her work, but many did not like the system and there was often quarrelling amongst them. A little wife might be keenly aware of her lesser status, while a main wife would become jealous if the husband paid too much attention to a younger co-wife. Sometimes a main wife would resent the very fact of her husband's taking another wife. Near Waitara in Taranaki, in the territory of Te Āti Awa, a woman named Te Rarawa-i-te-rangi protested with a waiata aroha when her husband, Te Kore-te-whiwhia, took a second wife after having promised not to do so.

E HOKA Ō RONGO

E hoka ō rongo, e hau i te rangi.
Hōmai kia pahua ki te ngutu mau ai,
He mea tangata hoki! Kei riri e Whenu',
He aha i riri ai ki te makau tangata?
Nāku anō ra taku whakaironga.

Ko te aha, e Kore, ō koha ki a au?
Ka eke 'nō au te puke ki Ōhuka!
E Ngata mā e, tukua kia haere!
Kāpā ianei kei te ohi anō,
E tau te kakare te tau o te manawa.
Nāu te kī nei, me taratahi au,
Ehara te hourua, kei eke i te papa
O Taumata-whārangi. He kōputunga ngaru
Pae ana ki te one, tēnei kei a au.

YOUR FAME SOARS UP

Your fame soars up, sounding in the sky —
Let it dart up to lips, and stay there!
A fine man indeed! Don't be angry Whenu',
Why be angry because of this man we love?
What I embrace is mine.

Kore, where is your regard for me?
I have climbed the hill at Ohuka.
Ngata and you others, let me go.
It's not as if I were still in my prime,
My heart-string is beating!
It was you who said I'd be the only one,
Not a double canoe, or it would mount the surface
Of Taumata-whārangi. A mass of sea-foam
Stranded on the beach, that's what I am.

TE RARAWA begins with ironical praise, telling her husband his fame is such that everyone should be talking about him; the implication is that he certainly deserves to be the subject of gossip. Then she appeals to Whenua-kura, the mother of Te Kore's new wife, asking her not to quarrel over him and pointing out that she herself has the prior claim. Next she appeals to Te Kore, saying she is growing old and implying that after the time they have spent together he owes her this koha, or token of his regard. Ōhuka must be a hill which becomes covered with snow, for its name means 'the place of snow'. In speaking of

Village life in the early 1840s.

herself as having climbed this mountain — probably a real one — she is saying poetically that she is taking upon herself the mountain's condition: her hair is turning white.

Te Rarawa then addresses a man named Ngata and those associated with him. These are apparently kinsfolk, probably her brothers. She asks to be allowed to leave her husband and return to them, saying that she is growing old and is greatly distressed. She reminds her kinsfolk that they themselves had stipulated (apparently before the marriage) that to avoid quarrels she was to be the only wife.

In the last lines Te Rarawa again complains about her circumstances, employing three traditional images in rapid succession. Women were often spoken of as canoes, and men as their paddlers; here, two co-wives are likened to a vessel made from two canoes lashed together. Quarrelling and fighting were often associated with stormy waters, and this is the significance of the reference to Taumata-whārangi — which, as George Grey tells us, is the name of 'the surf beaten shore . . . opposite the pa Puketapu near Waitara'; its crashing waves represent the fighting that would follow if there were to be a second wife. Finally Te Rarawa claims to be, as we might say, washed up. Abandoned and ageing, she is like sea-foam lying on the beach.

It is not known whether Te Rarawa managed to persuade her husband to change his mind, or if she went home to her relatives as she threatened. Quite possibly her song did achieve its purpose. Certainly the act of composing and singing it must have helped her to save face in a difficult situation. The very fact that it was handed down in oral tradition shows that those around her responded to her skilful poetry with interest and sympathy.

~5~
The Song about Turner's House

IN 1823 A WESLEYAN mission station was established in Te Tai Tokerau (Northland). There were already Church of England missionaries at the Bay of Islands, so the Methodists chose a site further north at Kaeo, up-river from the Whangaroa Harbour in the territory of Ngāti Uru. The leader of the mission, the Rev. Nathaniel Turner, had some knowledge of farming and another man, John Hobbs, was a carpenter and blacksmith. At Wesleydale, as they called their new home, Hobbs was responsible for the construction of buildings to accommodate the missionaries and the young Māori people who were living with them, a schoolhouse, a storehouse, a barn and outbuildings. Turner planted an orchard, grew vegetables, wheat and barley, and looked after the mission's cattle, goats and turkeys.

As well as trying to learn the language and communicate their message, the missionaries traded and gave away large quantities of axes, hoes, pots, knives and blankets, distributed plants such as wheat and peaches, dispensed medicine, and taught young people to read and write. Ngāti Uru welcomed these activities but paid little attention to the missionaries' preaching, for at that time they had no intention of abandoning their way of life, their beliefs and their gods. When the Methodists left Whangaroa early in 1827, driven out by tribal warfare, they had made no converts.

But although Wesleydale was abandoned and burnt to the ground, the memory of it persisted. Twelve years later, when Nathaniel Turner again visited Kaeo, he found that the site of the mission station, with its fruit trees and wild roses, was still known locally as Turner's kāinga, or settlement. As well, in a song which was composed some time after the mission station's destruction (probably in the 1830s, when the people of

The Rev. Nathaniel Turner, head of the mission station at Kaeo.

Te Tai Tokerau had become keenly interested in Christianity), the expression 'te whare i a Tāna', Turner's house, occurs as a way of referring to Christianity and the missions. Although the mission station itself had been destroyed, the idea of it functioned in this song as a poetic image.

E HŌHEPA E TANGI

E Hōhepa e tangi, kāti ra te tangi.
Me aha tāua i te pō inoi, i te pō kauwhau?
Me kōkiri koe ki te wai Hōrana
Kia murua te kino, kia wehea te hara, e tama ē.
Me kawe ake koe ki te whare i a Tāna
Kia tohutohungia ki te rata pukapuka —
Te upoko tuatahi, te upoko i a Kēnehi,
Te rongopai o Mātiu, kia whakamātau ai,
Kia kite te kanohi o te tinana, e tama ē.

YOU'RE CRYING, HŌHEPA

You're crying, Hōhepa, but don't cry any more.
What must we do on the night of prayers, the night of preaching?
You must leap into the waters of the Jordan
So that evil can be forgiven and your sins removed, my son.
You must make your way to Turner's house
And be taught the letters in the book —
The first chapter, the chapter of Genesis,
And the Gospel of Matthew, so you can learn,
So the eyes of your body can see, my son.

SOMETIMES in a song a poet addresses a weeping child, usually a boy, and speaks of a journey he must make to relatives who will give him recognition and support. Such songs generally belong to the genre known as oriori, though there are also some waiata which follow the verbal conventions of oriori and are called waiata whakaoriori, oriori-type waiata. This song celebrating Christianity may, therefore, be

In the ambitiously planned settlement there were buildings for accommodation, teaching and farming purposes. After four years the missionaries were forced to leave the district.

Ngāti Uru did not change their traditional beliefs, though they were glad to have trade goods readily available. At this time their leaders were two brothers, Te Āra (left) and Te Puhi.

either a waiata whakaoriori or an oriori. The name Hōhepa, or Joseph, shows that the person addressed is a Christian convert. The expression 'te wai Hōrana', the waters of the Jordan, refers to the episode in the Christian story in which Jesus was baptised in the River Jordan by John the Baptist; when Hōhepa follows the precedent established on this occasion he will, metaphorically speaking, enter the waters of the Jordan. When he receives further instruction from the missionaries, he will enter Turner's house — once again, metaphorically speaking. Although Turner's house was no longer standing, in this song it represents all mission stations, just as the River Jordan represents all baptismal fonts.

This use of imagery was in accord with Māori tradition and thought, in which important events, especially early ones, were very often regarded as having established precedents and patterns of behaviour that were to be followed by later generations. In the Christian tradition this also happens, to a degree; Jesus' baptism is an archetypal event, though less emphasis is placed upon the association of the Jordan and the font.

~6~

Lament for Tāmati Tara-hawaiki

FOR 15 YEARS the missionaries living in Te Tai Tokerau (Northland) made very few converts. Then there was a sudden change. In the early 1830s the people there became eagerly receptive to Christian teachings, and many were baptised. The faith spread to other parts of the country, there were thousands of converts, and by the early 1840s it was only in remote and relatively inaccessible areas that people held entirely to their old beliefs.

This break with the past came after some 20 years of social turmoil. Māori life had been greatly altered by the acquisition of new resources and technology, and diseases such as measles to which the people had no inherited resistance. There had been the unsettling realisation that they were not the only people in the world, that there were others elsewhere who behaved differently, and were rich. When the northern tribes acquired muskets there had been an intensification of warfare, though its ethos and satisfactions were not what they had been now that guns often made it impossible to know who had killed whom. Then the southern tribes began to catch up in the arms race. The northern tribes had reason to fear their revenge, and were in any case tired of war; many of their young men were now more interested in the profit to be made from selling pigs and potatoes to the growing numbers of Pākehā. By this time it came as a relief to realise that the missionaries' god punished wrongdoers after their death, and that unsettled scores could quite honourably be left for him to deal with. This god was clearly very powerful, for the Pākehā continued to flourish. They avoided wars, they did not die of diseases such as the measles, and they possessed an advanced technology.

One of their most impressive skills was their ability to read and write. When the missionaries began to share this knowledge, in the 1820s, the people were astonished and excited. To take speech from a human body and place it on a piece of paper seemed an almost magical thing, and old and young were eager to learn how it was done. Then the missionaries began translating and printing some of the books of the Bible, and these were read with intense interest. Soon, some of the first converts were taking the Gospel from their own region to other parts of the country, holding enthusiastically attended services morning and evening in raupō chapels built by their congregations. These lay preachers were known as mōnita, or monitors, a name given them by the missionaries when they had served as assistant teachers in the mission schools. But this apprenticeship lay behind them now. Monitors were men of standing who preached and taught often in virtual isolation, with only occasional visits from the missionaries. Christianity had become a Māori faith.

During this period of initial enthusiasm the death of a lay preacher was often mourned by his congregation with waiata tangi which celebrated

In the mission schools Māori men did much of the teaching. Later, some became lay preachers elsewhere.

their religion and honoured their teacher. Such a song was composed, probably in the 1830s, for Tāmati Tara-hawaiki, one of the earliest lay preachers amongst Ngāpuhi in the Far North.

KĀORE TE AROHA NO TĀMATI

Kāore te aroha no Tāmati, tē taka koe i a au!
E whakawhetai ana te pukapuka i te whare,
E kimi ana au ngā tūranga i te ata,
E rapu ana au ngā tūranga i waho ra,
I te tīmatatanga i te toru o Mātiu,
Te rongopai a Paora, hei ara mōhou.
Unuhia noatia taku manu noho puke,
Taku waka rehurehu ka tiu ki te uru.
Kei whea Tāmati, i nunumi ake nei?
Moe kē ana mai i roto i te waka iti,
He kāwhena tipua na ō tēina, na tō whānau,
Nāna i rauhanga, nāna i patupatu
Ki te whao a tawhiti! E pā i te nehu,
Tākiritia ra tō wairua ora!

The builders of village churches used mainly traditional materials and conventions, but were also influenced by European ideas.

Kia piki atu koe, uakina ake ra
Te tatau o te rangi, ka tapoko atu koe
Te ruma i a Ihu, kia inu atu koe
I te wai o te ora. Ko te wai tēnā
I whakahekea ai te toto o te Ariki —
Nāu i kōrero ki te ao Māori, ki a au na ē!

HOW GREAT IS MY LONGING FOR TĀMATI

How great is my longing for Tāmati — you do not fall from me!
The book is giving thanks in the house
And I am seeking you there in the morning,
Searching for you amongst those at the front
As the third of Matthew is begun,
And Paul's glad tidings that are a pathway for you.
My bird living in the hills is withdrawn,
My canoe soars to the west, dimly seen.
Where is Tāmati, who went so suddenly?
He sleeps apart in the little canoe,
A foreign coffin that your younger brothers and your family
Cunningly fashioned, striking it
With the chisel from afar. O father in the dust,
Let your living soul fly up!
Mount up, push aside
The door of the sky, and you will enter
Jesus' room, that you may drink
The waters of life. Those are the waters
For which the blood of the Lord flowed forth —
And it was you who spoke of this to the Māori world and me!

AT THE END of the first line it is the poet's longing which is addressed. Lamenting Tāmati's absence from his familiar place in the morning service, the poet speaks of St Paul, who in taking the Gospel to distant lands provided a precedent, a 'pathway' for Tāmati to follow. Next, two traditional images are employed to honour him. Probably he is likened to a bird because he was a fine orator who 'sang' sweetly; he is like a canoe because he has conveyed his people along the true path and because he is now, in death, travelling towards the setting sun. Perhaps, too, there is a reference here to the small canoe in which a body was often placed at a funeral, for this custom is referred to in the lines which follow — though the poet remarks with apparent pride that a modern coffin was in fact employed, one that had been shaped, moreover, with an iron 'chisel from afar'. The missionaries had persuaded their converts to make use of coffins. The poet is indicating that Tāmati's family have done all they can to honour him and follow Christian teachings.

Tāmati is seen as going up to Jesus in the sky. But while the idea of a room in the sky is a new one (houses had had no interior partitions), the expression 'te tatau o te rangi', the door of the sky, is traditional, and it had always been thought that the souls of some persons, especially the high-born, went to the sky rather than the underworld. The idea of drinking the waters of life may be new, though in some parts of the country it was believed that in the highest of the skies there existed 'te wai ora a Tāne', the living waters of Tāne, which were a source of human life. In traditional Māori thought, as in Christianity, the sky was a sacred, eternal realm, a place where death was unknown.

7

Te Whare-pōuri's Lament for Nuku-pewapewa

THE ACQUISITION of muskets led to a frantic arms race and sudden shifts in the balance of power. There was increased warfare, and there were large-scale migrations as disadvantaged tribes sought to escape from heavily armed neighbours and move to districts where muskets were available. From 1821 onwards, a number of allied tribes on the West Coast, under the leadership of Te Rauparaha, made their way southwards to the region around Raukawa (Cook Strait). Among them was the powerful tribe of Te Āti Awa from Taranaki.

One section of Te Āti Awa, led by Te Whare-pōuri, settled at Te Whanganui a Tara (Wellington Harbour). They defeated the occupants of the region, who had no muskets at all, they traded with the Pākehā ships now beginning to visit the area, and in the 1830s they joined in an attempted invasion of the Wairarapa.

This fertile region belonged to Ngāti Kahungunu, a most numerous people who also occupied the plains of Heretaunga (Hawke's Bay) and Wairoa. At this time the leader of the Wairarapa section of Ngāti Kahungunu was Nuku-pewapewa (or Nuku), a tall, handsome man who was a daring warrior, a tohunga and a poet. Nuku had spent many years defending Ngāti Kahungunu territory from the incursions of its enemies to the north-west, and to assist related tribes on the East Coast he had fought as far afield as Te Kaha. But Ngāti Kahungunu possessed very few muskets, and urgently needed them. So Nuku decided now to migrate with his people to Nukutaurua, at Te Māhia (Māhia Peninsula), where recently established whalers would trade muskets and ammunition for flax fibre, pigs and corn.

Te Whare-pōuri, portrayed speaking at Te Whanganui a Tara (Wellington Harbour). He pursued traditional objectives but also had to contend with the sudden arrival of large numbers of Pākehā settlers.

As soon as Nuku and his people moved north, Te Āti Awa and their allies occupied the Wairarapa. Nuku and his fellow rangatira from Heretaunga came with an army, but when the other leaders looked down from a high hill at all the fires of their enemies burning below, they declared that without muskets nothing could be done against so large a force. Nuku, however, made up his mind that he would put out the fires or die upon his own land. He and his 200 men went forward alone, and discovered that the enemy were not as strong as had been thought. At dawn they succeeded in trapping a number of people inside the houses where they had been sleeping; the only person to escape was the rangatira Te Whare-pōuri, who jumped from a cliff and was saved by a vine that broke his fall. No one was killed, for Nuku wished to make peace. He treated with great courtesy Te Whare-pōuri's wife and eldest daughter, who were among the captives, and in due course he sent them back to Te

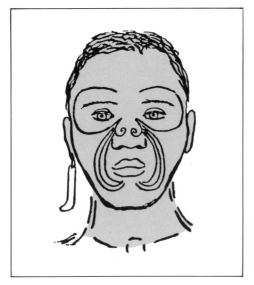

Legends tell of Nuku-pewapewa's exploits and some of his songs have survived. His moko (tattoo) was unorthodox in its design.

Whare-pōuri escorted by men who bore gifts of greenstone and fine cloaks as a token of the Ngāti Kahungunu desire for peace.

Te Whare-pōuri made an appropriate response. He persuaded his own tribe and nearly all his allies to retire from the Wairarapa, then he chartered a Pākehā ship and with a substantial entourage set sail for Nukutaurua to make peace with Ngāti Kahungunu and invite Nuku to return to his land. But on his arrival he learnt that Nuku was dead, drowned with many others in a storm at sea a short time before.

Te Whare-pōuri lamented the death of his former enemy with an old song, adapted for the occasion, in which the poet speaks first of the star Tariao, which shines in the early dawn. In a traditional image, the mourner with his eyes full of tears is likened to a star — for with their unsteady light, stars seem also to be weeping.

TĒRĀ TARIAO KA KŌKIRI

Tērā Tariao ka kōkiri kai runga.
Ko te rite i ahau e whakawhetū nei,
Te hua i te puku e kai momotu nei.

Wairua i tahakura, nōu nei e Nuku —
Kei te whakaara koe i taku nei moe
Kia tohu ake au ko tō tinana tonu.
Me he wai wharawhara te tuturu i aku kamo.
E tangi, e manu, kia mōhio Roto.
Ma te hau tonga e whiu i ahau
Ngā puke iri mai o Rangitoto i waho
Kia whāia atu ka wehe i ahau.
Tērā pea koe ka iria he maunga,
Ngā tai tangi mai o Manukau i raro,
Ki Ngāpuhi rāia, ki Wainuku-mamao,
Ki Morianuku. Te huri rawa mai
Tō wairua ora ki a au ki konei!

SEE WHERE TARIAO IS RISING

See where Tariao is rising over there.
It is my likeness: here I am like a star
With emotion devouring and rending within.
A soul visited me from death — it was yours, Nuku,
Waking me from my sleep,
Making me think you had come in the flesh.
Water falls from my eyelids, as from the perching lily.
Sing on, bird, bringing knowledge within.
The south wind must hurl me
Upon the high peaks of Rangitoto beyond
So I can follow my friend who is parted from me.
Perhaps you are lifted up on a mountain-top
With the tides of Manukau lamenting below,
Or with Ngāpuhi over there, at Wainuku-mamao
And Morianuku. Oh let your living soul
Turn back to me here!

AS OFTEN in poetry, the soul of the person who is mourned is said to have visited the singer in his dreams. The mourner's tears fall as freely as water from the perching lily; a bird brings a message from the beloved, or indeed may be the person himself, the body he now occupies. The singer traces the northward journey to Te Rēinga, the Leaping Place, which the dead man's soul will make, and he speaks of following him. Rangitoto Island and the Manukau Harbour, at Tāmaki, are landmarks often mentioned in such passages in laments. The Ngāpuhi tribe live in the Far North. Wainuku-mamao is a hill where the souls gaze back and send their last greetings to the land and the people they are leaving, and Morianuku is a place near the entrance to Te Rēinga.

Te Whare-pōuri's song became famous and was often sung, all the more so because it was associated with the peace which was now established between Ngāti Kahungunu and the tribes of the Raukawa region. This event took place in about 1840, at a time when the Treaty of Waitangi and the acceptance of Christianity were about to bring to an end the traditional way of life.

Rangitoto, in the Waitematā Harbour, was a famous landmark even to tribes living far to the south. By the time Te Whare-pōuri sang his farewell to Nuku-pewapewa, there were foreign vessels as well as canoes on the waters of the Waitematā.

8
Lament for Te Iwi-ika

IN MĀORI religious tradition the person responsible for introducing death into the world is Hine-nui-te-pō, Great-woman-of-the-night. According to a story told in the South Island, Tāne created the world by separating his parents, the sky and the earth, then went looking for a woman. At first he found women who were not human, and with them he created the different kinds of birds and plants. Then he made himself a human woman from the soil of Hawaiki. This woman bore him a daughter, whom he called Hine-tītama, and when she grew up he took her, too, as his wife. Among their children were two girls, Tahu-kūmea and Tahu-whakairo.

One day Hine-tītama discovered that her husband was also her father, and in great distress she rushed down to the underworld. Tāne followed and urged her to return, but she left him with these words: 'Return to the world, Tāne, to rear up our progeny, and let me go to the underworld to drag down our progeny'.

It is usually said that in the underworld Hine-tītama took a new name, Hine-nui-te-pō. Down there it is her task, accompanied by her daughters, to receive the wairua, the souls, of human beings when they die. But new generations keep growing up to replace these people in the world, for Tāne meanwhile creates new life. According to one tradition, to achieve this end he climbed up through the skies, encountering on his way the powerful figures who lived there, and in the highest of the skies he took possession of 'te wai ora a Tāne', Tāne's living waters. From these precious waters come the souls of newborn infants.

This story explaining the origins of death and of life was recalled by an unknown South Island poet in a waiata tangi for her husband.

Mohi Woods wrote down the words of the lament for Te Iwi-ika as dictated by his aunt Pinana at Waikouaiti in the early 1890s.

E KIMI ANA I TE MATE

E kimi ana i te mate o Te Iwi-ika,
Waniwani amu a wekuna i whakapiki
Ka reo o tini o te iwi o te ao.
Waiho kia mate ana te tangata —
Tāruatia nei e koe te mamae ki a au,
He tikanga huri kino i a au.
Whatungarongaro, ē, te tahu —
I ngaro tonu atu koe i ahau.
Hare ra i te ara whānui,
He rori ka tika i a Hine-tītama,
I a Tahi-kūmea, i a Tahu-whaera —
Ka tika te ara ki te mate.

Hua parau noa 'e tāne ki te whai atu —
Koia 'nō i tapoko atu ai ki rō te tatau
O te whare o Poutukutia, ko Poutererangi.
He oti tonu atu koe, e te tahu ei.
Hoki kau mai 'e tāne ki te ao nei,
Kōmiro kino ai tōna kākau, pēnei me au ē —
Momotu kino nei taku manawa
Kia a koe, e te tahu ei!
Whakapiki te haere a Tāne
Ki te raki i a Rehua i ruka,
Whakatika te haere a Tāne
Ki te raki i a Tama-i-wa'o,
Whakapiki titaha te haere a Tāne
Ki te rangi i a Rangi-whakaūpoko-i-runga —
Ka tūturu anō te kāhui ariki
Kai te mutuka o kā rangi!
Heke iho nei Tāne ki te whenua,
Ka kitea he mahara mo te tōhuatanga,
Ko tōna ika whenua, ka tipu he tāngata
Hei noho i te ao mārama ei.

SEEKING THE REASON

Seeking the reason for Te Iwi-ika's death
The voices of the multitudes in the world
Mount up, speaking bitterly.
Let the man be dead —
How you make my pain increase,
So that I turn about in sorrow!
Oh my husband is lost and gone —
You are lost to me forever.
Set out on the wide path,
The straight road of Hine-tītama,
Tahi-kūmea and Tahu-whaera,
The path that goes straight to death.
I had thought there would be a man to follow,
But he disappeared through the doorway
Of Poutererangi, Poutukutia's house.

Husband, you are gone forever.
When he visits this world again
His heart is cruelly twisted, as is mine —
My heart is cruelly broken,
Husband, because of you.
Tāne made his way upwards
To the sky of Rehua above,
Tāne made his way straight
To the sky of Tama-i-wa'o,
Tāne made his way up slantingly
To the sky of Rangi-who-forms-the-head-above —
The lordly company remains always
In the last of the skies!
Then Tāne came down to this land
And saw how it could be made fertile —
His mainland here — and people grew up,
To live in the world of light.

TE IWI-IKA'S WIFE first laments his death, twice speaking of him then addressing him (lines 4–5 and 7–8). She sends him on the path he will travel to the underworld, the home of Hine-tītama (who here retains her original name) and her two daughters, whom she calls Tahi-kūmea and Tahu-whaera. Poutererangi, a house usually said to belong to Hine-nui-te-pō, is here associated with a figure named Poutukutia.

She speaks of the times when Te Iwi-ika's soul returns to visit her at night, in dreams or perhaps a séance, and of the pain this causes them both. But she ends by affirming that life will continue, recalling for this reason the episode in the story where Tāne, returned from the underworld, set about his task of making the world fertile by going on a journey to the highest of the skies. Rehua and Tama-i-wa'o (or Tama-i-waho) are tapu, dangerous persons who inhabit the skies; Rangi-whakaūpoko-i-runga, or Rangi-who-forms-the-head-above, is a South Island name for Rangi, the sky father, who was believed to preside over the tenth, highest sky. 'Te ao mārama', the world of light, is an expression for the world of the living, as opposed to the underworld and darkness.

So having mourned and farewelled her husband, the poet brings her song to a positive conclusion. Though people die, others will replace them, and the world of light will be triumphant.

9

Kāhoki's Song for Petera Te Puku-atua

WHEN A WOMAN complained in a waiata aroha that the man she loved would not approach her, this did not necessarily mean that he was really indifferent to her. Women very often took the initiative in courtship, but they nevertheless had to maintain a certain feminine reserve. A poet's complaint of this kind was a socially acceptable way of honouring the man and professing her love while still managing to imply tactfully that it was his place, not hers, to make the move.

Rākapa Kāhoki was the daughter of Te Wehi-a-rangi, a rangatira of Te Arawa in the Rotorua district, and Te Rangi Topeora, a high-ranking woman of Ngāti Toa who was herself a poet. In 1844 the artist G. F. Angas met her and painted her portrait. She was, he later wrote, 'a woman of strong mind, with a proud and queenly bearing, and by her powerful talents, combined with her high birth, possesses an almost unlimited influence amongst her people.'

Some time after this, Kāhoki composed several waiata aroha for Petera Te Puku-atua of Te Arawa, whom she later married. One of her songs must have been composed at Ōhinemutu on Lake Rotorua.

E TĀ URU WAHO

E tā uru waho e wawara mai nei,
Mata' hehengi mai, kei te aroha au
Ki te anu hau-raro i tuku mai i te hiwi

Ki Ngongotaha ra. Tē hōhā noa
Taku nei titiro te puia i Whakahinga —
Tū mai i konā! Ma te ao tonga au
E kawe ki te rae o Tahere rāia —
Whai noa atu ai, ka huri atu na koe ī!

SEA WIND THAT MURMURS

Sea wind that murmurs towards me,
Gentle breeze, how I long
For a cold north wind coming down from the ridges
Over at Ngongotaha! I gaze unwearied
At the Whakahinga Geyser —
Remain behind me! The southern clouds
Will carry me to the brow of Tahere —
But still as I follow, you turn away!

Ōhinemutu, as seen from the lake in the years when Kāhoki composed her song. Approaching visitors are welcomed by people lined up on the shore and others standing in the warm thermal waters.

Petera Te Puku-atua (left) and Rākapa Kāhoki in their later years. After their marriage they lived with Kāhoki's relatives on the Kapiti coast.

IT WAS BELIEVED that a person's aroha, love, could be sent on the wind, so that a wind from the right direction could be a link between parted lovers. Kāhoki rejects a pleasant breeze coming from the coast and longs instead for a cold wind from Ngongotaha, the mountain immediately to the north. Ngongotaha is the tapu mountain of Ngāti Pēhi (or Ngāti Whakauē, as they later became), and their leading rangatira at this time was Petera Te Puku-atua; a tribe's mountain was often identified with its leading man, and Kāhoki must be referring here to Petera himself. It seems paradoxical that a north wind should be cold. Perhaps the implication is that Kāhoki would prefer even a rebuff from Petera to no contact at all with him.

Kāhoki farewells the Whakahinga Geyser, a well-known landmark, for she must pursue the man she loves. Tahere is a hill which is more or less an extension of Ngongotaha; the poet declares that the south wind will take her northward in this direction. Petera must have been living near

Tahere at the time, for she now addresses him (following a convention whereby a poet first speaks of a place, then addresses without further preliminary a person living there). The address to Petera reveals the subject of her song and so brings it to a fitting conclusion.

This short waiata aroha makes use of conventional elements with wit and finesse. Each of the three winds plays its part, as does each of the landmarks Ngongotaha, Whakahinga and Tahere. The poet creates a strong sense of movement towards her lover, then in the last line balances this with his action in turning away. Since this comes as a climax it receives a strong emphasis.

In reality there could have been few obstacles to the union of Kāhoki and Petera. Both belonged to the aristocracy of Te Arawa, and their marriage could not have been unexpected. The marriages of high-ranking persons were of great importance to their people, especially when they reinforced a tribal alliance, and there may well have been a general feeling that it was appropriate for Kāhoki, as an accomplished poet, to mark the occasion with waiata aroha. Her songs for Petera must have been sung widely for their poetry, and because of the event with which they were associated.

10
Lament for Ngaro

A BEAUTIFUL, high-ranking young woman, Ngaro was greatly loved by her people in the Hokianga region. When she died suddenly, apparently in the 1840s, they farewelled her with a waiata tangi composed by Patuwhakairi, a relative of her grandmother's generation. In her song the poet represents herself as mourning in the evening, a time traditionally associated with sorrow, and she identifies the evening star, disappearing behind the hills, with the girl who is lost to them.

TĒRĀ TE WHETŪ

Tērā te whetū me ko Rere-ahiahi
E torangi atu ana te pae ki Ati Rau.
Pai aha ra ia a au, i te ipo ka riro?
Engia ia koe ko taku taonga nui!
E hine kaitū, e hine kairere,
E hine kaikapo i te ranga-awatea,
I te hihi o te rā, ko 'e ti ka ngaehe
Roto o Awapoka, ō takanga tonu.
Ra pea koe he numinga, he kopanga —
Kāore, ka tū rewa te ngākau haere ē.

Whītikia tōu kahu i te ata ka whanake
Kia tuku atu ana ngā tira o te haere

Roro o te whenua, ka kitea ki runga ra,
Kia tangohia mai ko 'e kura a Māui,
Ngā mahi e pupuke i ō huānga rāia.
Me ko Hine na Rau, māna e rere atu —
Rukuhia iho ra ko 'e kuku moe toka,
Ko 'e ika kato rimu, kia piua iho
Hei kai ruru mai i te puni o te iwi,
I te puni wāhine, te nui a Titoro na ē.

Kei hea hoki ra ngā tai o te uru?
Ka ngaro hoki ra taku toko tai pari,
Taku toko tai timu e tū i waho ra,
Tūranga hoa i te one tai-tapa.
Whakaputaina ra, ko 'e waka tipi hau,
Kia rokohanga atu te au e mahora —
E kau i reira, he moana waiwai!
Rārangi noa ra te rāngai kūaka,
Kia tauhikohiko he pari tū waho.
I herea iho koe hei makau rawa atu.
I tapu i te aha tōu uru whatiwhati,
Tē hōmai ai hei mihinga ake
Mo Hine i te ao ē?

The handsome butterfish, or mararī, which lives in kelp and was often caught by women.

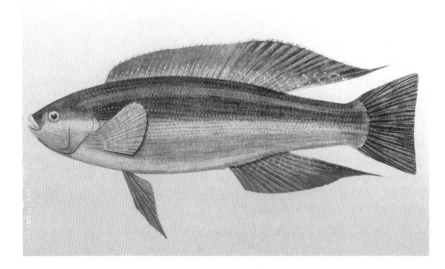

THERE IS THE EVENING STAR

There is the evening star setting
Over the ridge at Ati Rau.
What is left to me now my love is gone?
You were my great treasure!
Girl who is far distant, who fled,
Went so fast in the light of day,
The rays of the sun, you were a rustling cabbage tree
At Awapoka, where you used to roam.
Oh you disappeared, went suddenly —
You did not pause, your heart was set on going.

Put on your clothes as the dawn comes up
So your people can set out for the entrance
To the earth, and Māui's precious possession
Can be seen above and be gathered in,
The heaped-up produce of your relatives.
Rau's daughter must go speedily —
You must dive for mussels sleeping on the rocks

Godwits gather in late summer in large, restless flocks, in preparation for their northward migration. Their departure was sometimes seen as parallel to that of the souls as they set out for the underworld.

And catch the fish that pluck the seaweed, to be thrown down
As food to be strung together by your people,
The company of women, the multitude of Titoro.

Where now are the western tides?
She is gone, my prop of the rising tides,
My prop of the ebbing tides that lie beyond
The beaches by the sea, where her companions stand.
Go out in a canoe that glides in the wind,
Meet the current spread out before you,
Then swim, for it is the wide ocean!
Flocks of godwits are gathering,
Moving restlessly on the seaward cliffs.
You were bound to us, our best beloved.
Oh why was your fallen head so tapu
It was not given to us, who would have greeted you
With tears in this world?

THE PHRASE 'te ranga-awatea', the light of day, is a metaphorical expression referring to a time of peace. Patuwhakairi is speaking of the years that followed the Treaty of Waitangi, which in 1840 had brought most tribal fighting to an end. In another image, Ngaro is spoken of as a tree standing in a valley she had frequented.

As often with the poets of the Far North, Patuwhakairi recalls and relives the past. Speaking of Ngaro's parentage (Rau was either her father or her mother) and of her hapū, Titoro, she implores Ngaro to set out once more with the other women to harvest the kūmara (the precious possession of the mythical Māui), and to dive for mussels and catch the fish, such as butterfish, which feed on kelp close inshore. In Patuwhakairi's song Ngaro once again stands on the shore amongst her relatives.

Ngaro's presence is imagined as having sustained the very seas themselves; but she must now be sent on her last journey westward to the underworld, out in a small canoe on an ebbing tide. Finally she will leave her canoe, and swim. The migratory godwits, readying themselves on the cliffs for their own westward journey, show that it is time to go.

Sometimes the head of a person who had died was lovingly preserved and dried by the relatives so they could comfort themselves by greeting it with tears and waiata tangi. In the last lines Patuwhakairi regrets that with the arrival of Christianity this custom is now forbidden.

~11~
Mihi-ki-te-kapua's Song for Her Daughter

A FAMOUS POET of Ngāti Ruapani, Mihi-ki-te-kapua lived at Te Mātuāhu, an ancient pā on the northern shore of Lake Waikaremoana. In the 1850s, or perhaps the 1860s, her daughter, Te Uruti, married a man whose home was far to the north-west at Whakatāne, a small settlement near Te Whāiti. After a while Mihi heard that Te Uruti was being ill-treated by her husband. Unable to visit her — for the journey to Whakatāne was long and arduous, through dense beech forests and over precipitous mountains — she instead composed a waiata aroha addressed to her. This message must have passed from singer to singer and village to village until at last it reached Te Uruti.

Mihi's song begins with a new interpretation of a traditional idea which finds expression in many waiata. When a grieving poet could glimpse a hill near which a relative or lover was living, or perhaps see a column of smoke rising from the settlement, this was felt to establish a kind of contact with the absent person, and she would send her love on the wind towards it. When such a landmark was not visible, the poet might blame an intervening range for blocking her view; in this way she was at least able to mention a mountain lying in the general direction of her beloved. In her song Mihi allows herself poetic licence by blaming as an obstruction a tall kahikatea, a bird-spearing tree known as Te Waiwhero that stood near Te Whāiti. In reality the way was barred by the high ranges of the Urewera, notably the Huiarau mountains immediately to the north, but since Te Waiwhero was a well-known landmark this passage added interest to her song. It leads on to a reference to Te Uruti's home, and a loving greeting.

TIKETIKE RAWA MAI

Tiketike rawa mai Te Waiwhero —
Te turakina kia ngāwari,
Kia mārama au te titiro ē
Ki te rehu ahi o Whakatāne,
He tohu mai pea na te tau ē,
Ki' māha atu, ē, te ngākau,
Tēnei koe te hōkai nei ē
Ki tō moenga i awhi ai tāua ī!

Me i mātau ana i ahau ē
Ngā kōrero e takoto i te puka,
Me tuhituhi atu ki te pepa ē,
Ka tuku atu ki a Ihaka
Kia pānui a Te Uruti ē —
'E hine, tēnā koe!
Ka nui taku aroha ī!'

Kāore hoki, ē, te roimata,
Tē pēhia kei aku kamo.
Me he wai-rutu au ki Te Whāngaromanga ē,
Ko Haumapuhia e ngunguru i raro ra ī.

Tāwhai rawa mai, e hika!
Ko Ruawharo, te rite ra i te tipua,
E maka noa ra i ana pōtiki,
Tū noa i te one ko Matiu, ko Makaro,
Ko Moko-tua-raro ki tawhiti
I Ngaruroro ra, i Rangatira ra.

TE WAIWHERO IS TOO TALL

Te Waiwhero is too tall!
If it could be thrown down, laid low,
So I could see clearly
The haze from the fires at Whakatāne
Coming perhaps as a sign from my darling,
Soothing my heart,

The bird-spearing trees of the Urewera mountains were important landmarks. A rafter painting in the great house Te Whai-a-te-motu at Ruatāhuna.

Telling me you are striding swiftly
To your bed where we embraced!

If I had known
The speech that lies in books,
I would have written on paper
And sent it to Ihaka
So Te Uruti could read:
'Greetings to you girl,
I long for you so much!'

Oh alas for the tears
That cannot be kept from my eyelids.
I am like the water pouring down at Te Whāngaromanga,
Haumapuhia moaning below there.

Paitini Wī Tapeka of Tūhoe recorded Mihi-ki-te-kapua's song in the early 1890s for Elsdon Best, a Pākehā student of waiata.

O send your love to me, girl!
I am Ruawharo, like a demon,
Who threw away all his little ones
So that Matiu and Makaro stand always on the beach,
And Moko-tua-raro is far away,
Over at Ngaruroro and Rangatira.

IN THE SECOND verse, Mihi speaks of the new form of communication which was now available: if she had known how to write she would have given a letter to people travelling to Whakatāne, and a man named Ihaka (probably a lay preacher there) would have read it to Te Uruti. Although Mihi regrets that this did not happen, in her song she did in fact send her greeting.

From her home overlooking Lake Waikaremoana, Mihi could look across to the place on the southern shore where the waters of the lake disappear into an underground channel known as Te Whāngaromanga.

She likens her tears to the water pouring down this channel, and her moans to those of the woman believed to have created it in the early times.

According to tradition, a magician named Māhu once told his daughter, Haumapuhia, to draw water for him from a spring. When she refused to do so, the enraged father thrust her into the spring and she became a taniwha. She struggled to escape, forming the arms of the great lake, then she dug down into the earth, making the underground channel. When she came up to the light she turned into a rock that lies there still, and in the rushing waters her moans are still to be heard.

The last verse of Mihi's song is an adaptation of an ancient waiata, known in a number of versions, which refers to a myth set in Heretaunga (Hawke's Bay). After the tohunga Ruawharo arrived from the homeland of Hawaiki, he placed along the coast his three sons, turned to stone, as mauri (sources of fertility) in order to attract whales and other kinds of

Lake Waikaremoana, looking towards the southern shore.

fish to the region; Matiu is now a rock near Waikokopu Harbour, Makaro is at Aropaoanui and Moko-tua-raro at the mouth of the Ngaruroro River.

Because of his actions, Ruawharo is said in Mihi's song to be a tipua or demon, a person possessing awesome and sometimes terrible powers. Turning his sons into mauri was a miraculous and beneficent deed, yet at the same time a dreadful thing to do.

Ruawharo's irrevocable separation from his sons was an archetypal event, one which established a precedent and a pattern. Lonely parents parted from their children could identify themselves with Ruawharo, blaming themselves for their loss and gaining, perhaps, some comfort and dignity from this early precedent. In such a situation they might sing this little waiata, which was all the more poignant because of its familiarity. Mihi's use of it brings her own song to a fitting climax.

12

Tatai's Song for Te Toa-haere

IN ABOUT 1860, at Ōhinemutu on the southern shore of Lake Rotorua, the daughter of a rangatira of Ngāti Pēhi defied her father and her tribe by refusing to marry the man to whom they had promised her. Tatai Te Wai-atua had been made a puhi, a girl forbidden to have lovers and especially cherished by her people, and for good political reasons she had been betrothed to Hikairo, the leading rangatira of Ngāti Rangiwewehi on the northern shore of the lake. She must then have been about eighteen. Hikairo was very much older, probably in his fifties. Since he was married already, Tatai was to become his second wife, a position with inferior status.

But when a finely tattooed young rangatira named Te Toa-haere came visiting from Tauranga, Tatai fell in love with him. One night the two of them eloped, making their way in Tatai's little fishing canoe to Waikuta, a beach nearby. For a day and a second night they hid in a grove of trees there. Then they returned to face Tatai's angry people.

In taking a lover despite her betrothal and her status as a puhi, Tatai had broken the tapu placed upon her and could be felt to have insulted her own people, Hikairo, and Hikairo's people. To make matters worse, Te Toa-haere's tribe of Ngāiterangi were traditional enemies of the Rotorua tribes and some 25 years previously there had been a bitter war between them; while the 1840 treaty with the Pākehā had brought the fighting to an end, there were keen memories of unsettled scores. On Papa-i-Ōuru, the marae at Ōhinemutu, Tatai's father, brothers and elders strongly attacked Te Toa-haere and ordered him to leave next morning for Tauranga. Tatai was placed under guard to prevent her following him, and presently her father came to tell her the tribe had decided she was to

An ancestral figure from a storehouse on Mokoia Island, where Tatai and her people lived before they moved to Ōhinemutu.

marry Hikairo at once. Tatai told her father she had been spoilt for this purpose by Te Toa-haere and she would have him or no one. Then she climbed Te Puke-roa, the hill behind Ōhinemutu which was a traditional lookout. Weeping, she looked down at the place where she and her lover had been together, then she looked towards Tauranga beyond. As she watched the clouds moving towards her, she composed a song.

E MURI AHIAHI

E muri ahiahi takoto ki te moenga, ka rau aku mahara ei.
Tīkina mai, e Pāpā, ī, mātaia iho, tēnei anō au
Te kohi atu nei i aku tini mahara, pū ake ki te whare ei!

He kai au, e Pēhi, kia tohutohungia māu, e Hūkiki?
Riro te ngākau i a Te Toa-haere, waiho mōuka au.
Māku e mihi iho ki ō tāua moenga i nui o rangi ra ī —
Whai noa atu ana te one ki Waikuta, ka nunumi kino koe ei.
Māku e mihi atu te ao e rere mai nā runga o Mauao ī —
Kai raro Te Pakuru e hara mai nei, kai rawa i a au ihi!

SIGHING IN THE EVENING

Sighing in the evening, I lie on my bed and gather my thoughts.
Come and look at me, Father! Yes, here I am
Collecting my many thoughts, bent up in the house.
Am I food, Pēhi, to be kept for you, Hūkiki?
Te Toa-haere has my heart, and I won't give in.
I'll greet with tears the places we lay those many days —
I followed all the way to the beach at Waikuta, but you were gone, alas.
I'll greet with tears the clouds flying towards me from over Mauao.
Te Pakuru is below, coming this way — how love for him consumes me!

On Te Puke-roa, overlooking Lake Rotorua, Tatai composed her song as she gazed towards Tauranga, where her lover was living.

IN HER SONG Tatai appeals to her father, her tribe of Ngāti Pēhi, and Hikairo, to whom she had been betrothed (addressing him by his familiar name, Hūkiki). She makes use of traditional ideas and expressions: it was usually in the evening that people gave way to sorrow; unhappy persons often spoke of themselves as sitting crouched in their houses; and people collecting their thoughts were brooding over their wrongs. It was most demeaning for a woman to be spoken of as food for a man and Tatai uses this image to remind her tribe, and the man to whom she has been promised, that she cannot be treated like this.

Looking out from Te Puke-roa, Tatai could see the beach at Waikuta where she and Te Toa-haere had lain hidden. Te Toa-haere had passed this beach on his homeward journey, and Tatai speaks of having followed him, though in vain, as he did so. (This was poetic licence, as in reality her people had not let her out of their sight.) Then Tatai lifts her eyes to the clouds coming from the direction of Mauao, the mountain at Tauranga, and she greets them as being a link with Te Toa-haere. She ends by asserting that her lover (whom she speaks of now as Te Pakuru, using his familiar name) will return to her, and she reaffirms her love for him.

Tatai's song is an expression of emotion, and at the same time it is a rhetorical construct designed to persuade her listeners. On this level, the reference to Waikuta serves to remind her kinsfolk that her union with Te Toa-haere has already taken place. Similarly, the reference to Mauao and its clouds leads to the stubborn assertion that Te Toa-haere will return, and a final reminder that she is pining for him.

When Tatai returned to Ōhinemutu she sang her song to her woman friends and it soon became known to all. Meanwhile she wept and refused to eat, grieving constantly for her lover. And in the end she had her way; her family and her tribe, fearing she would die, sent for Te Toa-haere and the two were married. But Tatai and Te Toa-haere had only three years together at Tauranga. Then he died, and she followed soon afterwards. Her people brought her back, and she lies where she was born, on the heights of Mokoia Island in Lake Rotorua.

∽13∽
Rangiamoa's Lament for Te Wano

THE INCREASING numbers of Pākehā arriving and seeking land at first brought prosperity to the people who lived near enough to the towns to sell potatoes, pork and fish there. In many districts they began to grow wheat and grind it in their own flour-mills, gaining good prices for it in Auckland and Wellington. By 1850, flour from Māori mills was being exported as well to Australia and North America.

The Waikato tribes were among those who benefited in this way. Even in the Upper Waikato the people took their wheat, maize and potatoes down the river then overland to the Auckland markets, earning large sums of money and investing much of it in the purchase of horses, ploughs and drays. They also grew kūmara, pumpkins and other vegetables, and possessed hundreds of peach, apple, pear, plum, quince and almond trees. Since there was now much less fighting, they appeared to be leading a secure and comfortable existence.

But the Māori were under ever-increasing pressure from the Pākehā. To retain their land and their mana, and to establish an equal partnership with the Pākehā, many sought to unify the tribes under a king who would be the Māori equivalent of the Pākehā Queen. After much debate, in 1858 a high-ranking Waikato rangatira, Pōtatau Te Wherowhero, was made king by an assembly of rangatira representing most of the major tribes in the country. On his death two years later he was succeeded by his eldest son, Matutaera, later known as Tāwhiao.

The Government refused to recognise the Māori King or grant the Waikato people the measure of self-government they demanded, while in Auckland the settlers became ever more impatient for land. Then in 1863

Governor Grey found the excuse he wanted when Taranaki men fighting Government troops over a disputed sale of land were supported by some of Tāwhiao's followers. Grey wanted to destroy the King Movement and 'open up' for European settlement the rich lands which the Waikato tribes would not sell. He had a military road constructed southwards from Auckland, and on 12 July 1863 the first of the Government troops moved into the Waikato. The King Movement tribes fought bravely and resourcefully for nine months, but were finally defeated in 1864 at Ōrākau in the Upper Waikato. More than a million acres of Waikato land were confiscated by the Government.

Driven from their homes, Tāwhiao and many of his people took refuge with their Ngāti Maniapoto allies in the rugged country to the south, where they remained for many years. Others went elsewhere. At Rangiaowhia in the Upper Waikato (near the site of the present town of Te Awamutu), a section of Ngāti Apakura set out for Taupō. When they

Gunboats on the Waikato River took Government troops into the interior. An engagement at Meremere in October 1863.

reached Mt Tītīraupenga, a man named Te Wano asked his kinsmen to climb the mountain with him so that he could look a last time upon the lands near his home. They did so, and on the summit Te Wano died. His people buried him there, then made their way onwards. At Taupō they settled amongst Ngāti Tūwharetoa at Waihī and Tokaanu, though some later died in an epidemic.

A woman named Rangiamoa, a cousin of Te Wano, lamented her people's sufferings and Te Wano's death in a waiata tangi which became famous and is still widely sung. She speaks of the wind as coming from the north, the direction in which lie Paerau (the underworld, to which go the souls of the departed) and also Rangiaowhia, their former home. She recalls the years of plenty before the war, and she farewells Te Wano ('Tīrau is a shortened form of Titīraupenga).

E PĀ TŌ HAU

E pā tō hau, he wini raro, he hōmai aroha ī
Kia tangi atu au i konei, he aroha ki te iwi
Ka momotu ki tawhiti, ki Paerau. Ko wai e kite atu?
Kei hea aku hoa i mua ra, i te tōnuitanga ī?
Ka hara-mai tēnei, ka tauwehe, ka raungaiti au ī.

E ua e te ua, e tāheke koe i runga ra ē.
Ko au ki raro nei riringi ai te ua i aku kamo.
Moe mai, e Wano, i 'Tīrau, te pae ki te whenua
I te wā tūtata ki te kāinga koua hurihia.
Tēnei mātou kei runga kei te toka ki Taupō,
Ka paea ki te one ki Waihī, ki taku matua nui
Ki te whare kōiwi ki Tongariro, e moea iho nei.
Hoki mai e Roto ki te puia nui ki Tokaanu,
Ki te wai tuku kiri o te iwi e aroha nei au ī.

THE WIND BLOWING SOFTLY

The wind blowing softly from the north brings longing,
And I weep. My longing is for my people

Te Heuheu Tūkino (Mananui) with his younger brother Iwikau. Their successor in the 1860s was Mananui's son Horonuku.

Gone far off to Paerau. Who can find them there,
Where are my friends of those prosperous times?
It has come to this, we are separated and I am desolate.

Rain down, rain, pour down from above.
Here below you, I shower rain from my eyes.
Wano, sleep on at 'Tīrau, the barrier that hides
The land near the home we have abandoned.
Here we are on the rock at Taupō,
Stranded on the shore at Waihī with my great father
In his burial place on Tongariro, whom I see in dreams.
Within, I return to the great hot springs at Tokaanu,
The bathing waters of the people for whom I long.

AFTER SPEAKING of Ngāti Apakura's lost home and those who are gone, Rangiamoa turns to their present situation and acknowledges the assistance and the mana of two leading sections of Ngāti Tūwharetoa. First she speaks of the people on the western shore of the lake; the expression 'te toka ki Taupō', the rock at Taupō, refers to the high cliffs along the western shore and implies that the people who live there possess rock-like strength and resolution. Placing herself under their protection, she mourns the death of their great rangatira Te Heuheu Tūkino (Mananui), speaking of him as her 'matua nui', great father. Te Heuheu and many of his tribe had died in a landslide nearly 20 years previously and his bones had been interred upon Tongariro, the tapu mountain that Rangiamoa now acknowledges. She then turns to the section of Ngāti Tūwharetoa who were living in the Tokaanu district to the south, where the leading rangatira at this time was Te Herekiekie, and quoting from an old song she celebrates another landmark of great mana, the area of hot springs and other thermal activity near the mouth of the Tokaanu River. Having mourned the past, she faces the future.

14

The Exile's Lament

AFTER THE TARANAKI tribes had been defeated by the Government in the early 1860s, they listened to the prophet Te Ua Haumene when he told them that the archangel Gabriel had revealed to him the true form of Christianity, known as Hauhau, and that Tama Rura, or Son Ruler (the name he gave to Christ) would give them victory over the Pākehā and come at the millenium to rule the world. Te Ua's Hauhau faith was received with great enthusiasm throughout the West Coast, and his emissaries carried the message to distant tribes.

In the Tūranga (Gisborne) region, on the other side of the island, many of the people became Hauhau and a strong pā was built and occupied at Waerenga-a-Hika. In November 1865, Government forces laid siege to it. The men inside spent several days praying, then they charged out with their right hands uplifted, as they had been taught, to turn aside the bullets. But their faith did not prevail. More than 100 people were killed, many more were wounded, and some 400 were taken prisoner. Valuable land at Tūranga was seized by the Government in retaliation for this act of rebellion.

Many of the prisoners were sent by ship to Ahuriri (the Napier district), where the Superintendent of the Province of Hawke's Bay, Donald McLean, decreed that they should be banished to Wharekāuri (the Chatham Islands). The exiles must have sung songs lamenting their fate, but the lament most widely known was composed and sung in Tūranga, the region from which they had been deported. The poet, Tawapiko, speaks as if he himself were one of the captives. He traces their journey to Wharekāuri, and describes their unhappiness.

KA TŪ AU, KA KORIKORI

Ka tū au, ka korikori.
Ka puta te rongo o Taranaki e hau mai nei,
Ka toro taku ringa ki te atua nui o te rangi e tū iho nei,
Ko Tama Rura! Ka mate i te riri i Waerenga-a-Hika,
I te toru o Maehe i whiua ai au ki runga i te kaipuke,
Ka tere moana nui au, ngā whakaihu ki Waikawa ra,
Ka huri tēnei te riu ki Ahuriri, e te Makarini,
Ka whiua atu au ki runga ki a Te Kēra. Au e noho nei,
Ka tahuri whakamuri, he wai kai aku kamo e riringi nei.
Whanganui, Whangaroa, ngā ngaru whakapuke kai Wharekāuri!
E noho, e te iwi, tū ake ki runga ra, tiro iho ki raro ra.
Āwangawanga ana te rere mai a te ao na runga i Hangaroa —
I ahu mai i Tūranga, i te wā kāinga kua wehea —
No konei te aroha, e te iwi! Kua haere nei
Kūpapa, e te iwi, ki raro ki te maru o te Kuini
Hei kawe mo tātau ki runga ki te oranga tonutanga.
Kāti ra ngā kupu e makaa i te wā i mua ra.
Tēnā ko tēnei, e te iwi, whakarongo ki te ture Kāwana
Hei whakapai ake mo te mahi a Rura, nāna nei i raru ai ē.

Guarded by soldiers, Hauhau men captured in the fighting on the East Coast await their fate at Ahuriri.

I STOOD UP AND I ACTED

I stood up and I acted,
Taranaki's news came resounding to me here
And my hand went out to the great god of the sky that stands above,
Tama Rura! He was defeated in the fighting at Waerenga-a-Hika.
On the third of March I was flung on board ship
And sailed the broad ocean — the headlands of Waikawa,
Then I turned, McLean, to the Ahuriri Plain!
I'm flung on to the *St Kilda*, and sitting here
I turn and gaze back, water pouring from my eyes.
Whanganui, Whangaroa, the waves mounting up at Wharekāuri!
My people sitting here, rise up, look to the north.
The clouds flying towards us over Hangaroa bring grief,
They come from Tūranga, the home we're parted from,
Causing such longing, my people. We are lying low now,
My people, under the shelter of the Queen
That will bring us to prosperity.
Enough of the words thrown about in the past!
Instead, my people, obey the Governor's laws
So we can put right Rura's deed that brought all this trouble.

TAWAPIKO first recalls the events that led to the fighting, speaking with disrespectful irony of Tama Rura, whom the men at Waerenga-a-Hika had trusted. He then describes the voyage to Ahuriri, and on to Wharekāuri; on the way to Ahuriri the prisoners passed Waikawa (Portland Island), off Māhia Peninsula. Donald McLean is addressed because he was responsible for their banishment; the *St Kilda* is the sailing ship in which they were transported to Wharekāuri, and Whanganui and Whangaroa are places there. The poet represents the exiles as weeping at the sight of the clouds moving towards them from the direction of their home, and he reminds his listeners that to avoid further suffering they have now rejected Tama Rura and accepted instead Queen Victoria's rule and the Government's law.

Among the prisoners sent to Wharekāuri there was one man, Te Kooti Rikirangi, who had fought for the Government, not against it. He had been accused of sympathising with the rebels but nothing had been proved, and he was sent off with the rest mostly to get rid of him, for he had a

The prophet Te Kooti Rikirangi, to whom the exile's lament is often attributed.

reputation as a troublemaker. At Wharekāuri he experienced a revelation during an illness and he afterwards began promulgating his own interpretation of the Bible. In 1868 he led a revolt, seized a ship, and brought his followers back to Aotearoa. They landed near Tūranga and fought their way inland into the densely forested Urewera mountains, where for three years, with the support of the Tūhoe people, they evaded the Government forces sent against them. They then took refuge in Te Rohe Pōtae (the King Country), the territory of Ngāti Maniapoto and King Tāwhiao. There they remained, safe from the Pākehā, until the Government for political reasons pardoned Te Kooti in 1883.

Te Kooti's influence as a prophet was greatest in the Bay of Plenty and the Urewera, but his name was honoured by tribes in other regions also. In developing and promulgating his teachings he drew upon every body of tradition available to him, in particular the Bible, Te Ua's teachings, and Māori poetry. While he was not himself a poet he made clever use of existing songs, modifying them where necessary to convey his ideas, and these adapted songs were often thought to have been composed by him. It is not known whether he ever sang Tawapiko's song, but certainly it was sometimes attributed to him. Because he eventually renounced violence

James Kerry-Nicholls and his guide are welcomed at Ruakaka. The people there sang the lament to celebrate Te Kooti's teachings.

and made his peace with the Government, the last lines presented no obstacle to this interpretation.

In the year in which Te Kooti was pardoned, an Englishman named James Kerry-Nicholls visited Ngāti Maniapoto's territory and in the remote settlement of Ruakaka, west of Mount Ruapehu, heard this song sung and attributed to Te Kooti. Ruakaka was on the banks of the turbulent Manganuioteao River, in 'a fine, open valley, sunk like a pit, as it were, in the heart of a mountainous region, where enormous forests stretched away as far as the eye could reach on every side'. The people there were Hauhau. Kerry-Nicholls stayed with them for a couple of days, and he learnt something of their beliefs.

He found they were no longer sure their faith would save them. One old man, 'who had been a noted fighting-chief during the war . . . spoke out frankly, and said, "At one time I thought there were two saints in the islands — Tāwhiao and Te Whiti — and I waited a long time to see if they would be taken up to heaven in a chariot of fire, but I have waited so long that I am tired, and now I think that there are no saints in heaven or on earth".' An old chieftainess 'who was always a good talker, and displayed at all times a facetious spirit, laughed heartily at [this] admission . . . and then, looking us full in the face, she exclaimed . . . "We believe in nothing here, and get fat on pork and potatoes." This brought down roars of laughter from the assembled Hauhaus.'

Yet despite such claims the people were 'always ready to sing Hauhau chants to the glorification of Te Whiti and Te Kooti, who appeared to be [their] presiding deities . . . At night, when the wind and rain raged without, and the river rushed through its rock-bound channel with a noise like thunder, both men and women would chant these wild refrains in droning, melancholy notes, but in perfect harmony, the airs in most cases being exceedingly pretty and touching.'

One of the songs sung by the people of Ruakaka was the old lament for the exiles at Wharekāuri. Now thought to have been composed by Te Kooti, it was understood as being a recital of the prophet's sufferings and at the same time an affirmation that he and his people, although they were not now fighting the Government, would survive and prosper.

The song is still sung today, especially by members of Te Kooti's Ringatū faith in the Urewera and the Bay of Plenty, and it still has this significance.

15

Puhiwāhine's Song about Her Lovers

RIHI PUHIWĀHINE, a high-spirited, talented woman of Ngāti Maniapoto and Ngāti Tūwharetoa, was born near Taumarunui in about 1816. Her mother was a song-leader and composer, and at an early age Puhiwāhine became an accomplished performer of waiata and pātere. As a young woman she paid many visits with her Taupō people to other tribes, and with her beauty and her gifts as a performer and composer she attracted the attention of leading rangatira. Some she rejected, and some she did not, but on several occasions she fell in love and wanted to marry, only to be taken away by her brothers because her lover was already married or betrothed and they did not wish their sister to have the lower status accorded a second wife. She travelled a great deal, visiting communities as far away as the South Island, but for a long time she pined for two men in particular, her first lover Eruera (or Hauāuru) and her distant relative Te Māhutu Te Toko.

Finally, in the early 1840s, Puhiwāhine married a German immigrant named John Gotty. From about 1850 until 1863 Gotty was the proprietor of the Rutland Hotel in Wanganui, and there, as Pei Te Hurinui tells us, her 'sparkling wit and charm made her a popular figure in the town ... Puhiwahine became a lady of fashion, and in European society she was a lady to the manner born.'

As a guest at gatherings of the river tribes at Pūtiki, near Wanganui, Puhiwāhine was often urged to sing her songs.

> The people never tired of hearing her sing, and her artistic temperament responded gladly to the delighted shouts which her

Puhiwāhine (*c.* 1816-1906) was famous for her talents as a performer and composer.

performances evoked. Some of her women friends, and the chiefs, too, when they got to know her well, were prone to tease and provoke her about her youthful escapades. It was as the result of this that she composed one of her well-known songs. It is a class of song in which the composer seeks to make commonplace any oblique references to his or her behaviour. But Puhiwāhine in her song outbids all others, and she gives a long catalogue of her love affairs and her many flirtations.

KĀORE HOKI KOIA TE RANGI NEI

Kāore hoki koia te rangi nei,
Whakawairuhi rawa i ahau!
Taku tinana kau te noho nei,
Aku mahara kei te *purei* atu.

Ka pikitia te pikinga i Herepū,
Taiheke tonu ko Paripari,
Taurakuraku ki a Tanirau —
Kauaka iara, na Kataraina!

Ka tika tonu, ē, taku haere,
Ōrahiri — ko koe, Anatipa!
Kei rīria mai e Huriana,
Ka nui rahi rawa te whakamā!

Ahu tonu atu au ko Waipā —
Kei Rangitoto, ko koe ra Eruera!
Mere Tuhipo, he wawata kau atu
Te mea ra nāna i tuatahi.

Ka *hitimitia* mai e Marata!
Me ranga tonu te *wake* ki Kihikihi,
Kei reira tika hoki Maniapoto,
Ko Rahurahu, ko Raureti.

Ka ranga tonu te *wake* ki Kāwhia,
Kei Ahuahu hoki ko Te Poihipi —
Engari tērā, kua moe māua
Riterite rawa hoki ki te *mārena*!

Ka hoki muri mai taku haere,
Ka tomokia te whare o Ripeka —
Ehara, e kui, he tahakura nāku
Tauawhi-pō au ko Reihana!

Ka mutu hoki au ki te tai raro,
Ka hoki mai au ki Tūhua,
Ka noho au te kei o taku waka,
Ka tukutuku ngā ia ki Paparoa.

Kei raro iti atu ko Tōpine —
Tirohia kautia ake tērā,
E wehi ana au, he rangatira —
Kāore iara, he koroheke!

Konihi tonu te tere a taku waka,
Ka ū ana ko Waipākura,
Tauawhiawhi ki a Te Tahana —
Matarorangi, kei riri mai koe!

Ahu tonu ake au ko te *pāpara*,
Taurakuraku ki a Meiha Keepa —
E kui, Mākere, kei riri noa koe.
Kua kino koe, kua nui ō hē!

Kei te *pīti* hoki i Whanganui,
Ma Te Oti Kati au e pēhi mai —
'Pi owha, ko wē, ko hōma,
Piri pi koaeata! Hu toro iu, kamu mai perehi?'
Hei ha, hei ha, hei!

OH WHAT A DAY

Oh what a day this is,
It makes me feel so listless!
Only my body remains here,
My thoughts go playing away.

I'll climb the hill at Herepū,
Then right down to Paripari
And scratch with Tanirau —
Oh don't do that, he's Kataraina's!

I'll go on my way, straight on
To Ōrahiri — and you, Anatipa!
I'd better not, or Huriana will be angry
And I'll be so ashamed.

On I'll go to Waipā —
At Rangitoto you are there, Eruera!
Mere Tuhipo, I'm only daydreaming
About the one that was the first.

The Rutland Hotel, an important social centre in Wanganui, was owned for some years by the poet's husband.

Now Marata will hit me!
I must keep on walking to Kihikihi,
And there make for Maniapoto,
Rahurahu and Raureti.

I'll keep on walking to Kāwhia,
For at Ahuahu there's Te Poihipi —
He was the one, we lived together
Just as if we were truly married!

I'm on my way back now,
Entering Ripeka's house —
Not really, madam, it was only a dream
When I embraced Reihana in the night!

I'm finished in the north,
I'll come back to Tūhua
And sit at the stern of my canoe,
Going down the rapids at Paparoa.

Tōpine lives just below there,
He's only to be looked at,
I'm afraid of him, he's a rangatira —
No, really it's that he's so old!

My canoe goes gliding on
And lands at Waipākura.
There Te Tahana and I will embrace —
Matarorangi, don't be angry!

I'll keep on going to the pub,
And there scratch with Major Keepa.
Don't be too angry Mākere,
You're bad enough yourself!

Now to the Whanganui beach,
And George Gotty will be down on me —
'Be off, go away, go home,
Please be quiet! Who told you, come to my place?'
Hei ha, hei ha, hei!

L IKE MANY composers of waiata whaiāipo, Puhiwāhine sends herself in her song on a journey to visit former lovers and other men she admires. In speaking of them she also refers as a matter of politeness to their wives, first naming a man then mentioning or addressing his wife. Her journey begins near Te Kuiti, where she claims the great rangatira Tanirau will be her lover (scratching with a fingernail was a lover's overture often referred to in tradition). Tanirau, or Taonui, had once shown an interest in Puhiwāhine but there had been no affair, and since he was married her brothers had quickly removed her. At the nearby village of Ōrahiri, Te Anatipa had once made advances to her but he had received no encouragement and there had been an angry outburst from his wife. Near the Rangitoto Range at the headwaters of the Waipā, Eruera, or Hauāuru, had been her first lover and she had very much wanted to marry him; Mere Tuhipo and Marata are two of his wives. There had been no affairs with the next men mentioned, Rewi Maniapoto and his cousins Rahurahu and Raureti, but there had been one with Te Poihipi at Kāwhia, and again she had wanted to marry him. The rangatira mentioned in the rest of the song are included simply as being the great men in their regions: Reihana or Wahanui in the territory of Ngāti

Tanirau, or Taonui, of Paripari near Te Kuiti.

Rewi Maniapoto of Kihikihi.

Reihana, or Wahanui, of Hangatiki.

Tōpine Te Mamaku of the upper Whanganui.

Major Keepa (Kemp) of the lower Whanganui.

Five of the leading rangatira whom Puhiwāhine speaks of in her song. They were photographed some years afterwards.

Maniapoto to the north, and the others on the Whanganui River, which Puhiwāhine speaks of herself as descending. In the upper Whanganui the high chief Tōpine Te Mamaku was then a very old man, as Puhiwāhine remarks. Further down the river, the leading rangatira was Te Tahana, and in the lower reaches there was the well-known leader Major Keepa (Kemp). The pub is the Rutland Hotel, until 1863 the poet's home.

Puhiwāhine enjoyed using Māori versions of English words and phrases, and most of the ones in this song must have been employed consciously and for witty effect; they are therefore italicised in the Māori text. Pei Te Hurinui tells us that 'although she became quite proficient in English . . . there was always a tendency on her part to "maorify" English words, and as a loving mother she delighted in teasing her two sons by exaggerating her speech in this way'. In the last verse she teases George Gotty, her younger, favourite son, by pretending he will reject her, addressing her in English as he does so; it sounds as if George were living on land near the Whanganui beach.

This light-hearted song does not mention the man Puhiwāhine had perhaps loved most of all. She had met Te Māhutu Te Toko at a tribal meeting at Whatiwhatihoe and they had become lovers, but she was taken away by her brothers, who would not consent to her marrying him. This was probably because he was already married, so that her status would have been that of a second wife. Puhiwāhine composed a waiata aroha for Te Māhutu, one that is still often sung today, but apparently she could not bring herself to joke about him.

Her waiata is transitional in style. Apart from speaking of scratching, the poet includes no sexual references and images of the old kind, and this may be due to her Christianity (she was a Catholic). It may not have been entirely a matter of propriety; very likely she did not think in those terms, exactly. Using a modified form (her short, regular verses must be influenced by English ones), Puhiwāhine names many more people than usual and gives a more extended commentary. The encounter she imagines with her son, and the deliberate introduction of English words and phrases, are other new elements.

Pei Te Hurinui remarks that

> The song owes its survival to the fact that the descendants of those mentioned in it have had the verses handed down to them by their forebears. Some present-day families know only the verse in which one of their line is mentioned. It is no exaggeration to say that mention of an ancestor in this song is like a citation for military honours.

He also records a notable occasion on which part of her song was sung in Puhiwāhine's presence. In 1886, when she was aged about 70, she attended a Land Court sitting held at Ōtorohanga to investigate titles to tribal lands in the area. Hauāuru, the great rangatira who had been her lover some 50 years before, was the principal witness for Ngāti Maniapoto. During an adjournment of the court he challenged the counter-claimants to quote a song in support of their claims. When there was no response, Hauāuru, acknowledging Puhiwāhine's presence with a respectful gesture, began to sing her waiata whaiāipo. 'Puhiwahine took it as a challenge and soon she had risen to her feet and joined him in the singing; but remaining in her place some paces away.' At the fourth verse, which speaks of Hauāuru (or Eruera), she accompanied her singing with a pūkana, a performer's grimace, in his direction. For the line

>Kei Rangitoto, ko koe ra, Eruera

>At Rangitoto you are there, Eruera

'she raised her voice to a higher note and with quivering hands she struck a graceful pose reminiscent of her younger days.' The two singers ended with the lines

>Mere Tuhipo, he wawata kau atu
>Te mea ra nāna i tuatahi.

>Mere Tuhipo, I'm only daydreaming
>About the one that was the first.

16
Football Song

BY THE 1880s rugby football had become popular and was a focus for much friendly tribal rivalry. Ngāti Tamawhiti, a hapū of Ngāti Tūwharetoa at Moawhango in the Pātea region near Taihape, were often visited by football teams and their supporters from other hapū of Ngāti Tūwharetoa, and one of these groups made up a song praising the home team. Later it was sung in other places, adapted to new circumstances.

EI, TĀKIRI MAI KO TE ATA

Ei, tākiri mai ko te ata,
Ka puta atu ki waho, ka titiro noa atu
Ki waenga i te whīra te pōhututanga mai
O te karapu a Pine ī!

Ei, tērā te karapu
Nōu na, e Rima, te kori ra i roto
I te riu o Pātea. He rongo whutupōro
I tere papae ai! Auraki kau au
Ki te rapu i ngā ture. Ko koe na, e Tea,
Te tangata i mōhio ki ngā ture hōu nei,
Hei ako i ahau. I rere tō waewae
Ki te kiki i te pōrō ī!

Ei, he huinga, he minenga
Ki te purei i Pātea! Ka kitea i reira
Tō mōhiotanga, ka kitea i reira
Taku kuaretanga. Tīraha, e te karapu,
Kia tirohia atu te rere mai o te kiki
A Ngāti Tamawhiti ī!

EI, WHEN DAY DAWNS

Ei, when day dawns
We set out, and see right ahead
In the middle of the field, Pine's club
Thundering towards us!

Ei, that's your club,
Rima, leaping about in
The Pātea valley. Your football fame

As well as exchanging visits within Aotearoa, Māori football teams were soon going overseas. In 1888 this side toured Britain, playing 107 games and winning 84 of them.

The meeting-house Whitikaupeka was built at Moawhango at about the time that the football song was composed.

Is soon spread abroad! In vain I go about
Seeking the rules. Tea, you're the man
Who knows these new rules
And can teach me. Your foot flew
To kick the ball!

Ei, a meeting, a gathering
To play at Pātea! Your knowledge was seen there, my ignorance
Was seen there. Lie down, club,
And watch the flight of the ball kicked by
Ngāti Tamawhiti!

THE PRACTICE referred to in the last sentence was an old one. Men assessing the performance of a haka would sometimes lie down to get a better view of the dancers' feet.

Other clubs adapted the song to their own use by changing the names, and it passed from one district to another. It is asked for at tangihanga when someone mentioned in it has died.

~17~
Song for Te Whiti

WHEN THE TOWN of Parihaka was founded by Te Whiti-o-Rongomai the Taranaki tribes were desperate, having lost most of their fertile lands despite their determination not to sell them. An unscrupulous Government had first provoked a war through the wrongful seizure of land at Waitara and then, after winning, 'punished' the tribes for having defended themselves by confiscating most of their territory. More fighting followed when the people accepted Te Ua's Hauhau faith, thinking it would ensure their victory.

At Parihaka, Te Whiti established a community and for 40 years, until his death in 1907, led his people in a programme of passive resistance. To assert their rights of ownership, Te Whiti's men ploughed, fenced and cultivated the disputed ground; taken prisoner, they went uncomplainingly to gaol. Te Whiti himself, with his fellow leader Tohu, spent 16 months in prison without trial after the Government in 1881 sent a military force to destroy Parihaka and disperse its inhabitants.

Parihaka was rebuilt after this attack and it continued to provide the Taranaki tribes, and others elsewhere, with a source of hope and a focus for their aspirations. Contributions of cash and food poured in from around the country, and the large numbers of supporters who visited Parihaka received lavish hospitality. The spirit of resistance was inculcated and strengthened with impressive performances of waiata, haka and poi chants in which the poets drew upon Māori tradition and quoted from biblical writings and the prophecies of Te Whiti.

One waiata, probably composed in the early 1890s, was recorded in a family manuscript book in Ōtakou (Otago). It appears to have been

Te Whiti addresses a Parihaka meeting in 1881.

composed by people living at a distance from Parihaka, and may well be by a South Island poet. Ngāi Tahu were strong supporters of Te Whiti, having themselves suffered greatly through the illegal seizure of land.

E NOHO ANA I TE WHARE

E noho ana i te whare, e matatū kōkirikiri ana,
Te rere mai a te ao, he hōmai aroha ki ahau
Mo te iwi ra ka rutua ki te mate.
E Te Āti Awa, kia ara na ki te kimikimi
I te ara o te tikanga e mahia mai nei
E Te Whiti mā, kia hoki mai ai te mauri ki ahau ī!

Ka hora, ka hora te tēpu o Te Niho.
E pā, haria mai ngā ture nui, e au!
Me pēwhea tatou kia ora ai?
Me kawe rawa atu ki Parihaka ra,
Te whare iara i a Nohomairangi.
Engari Te Whiti kua kite i ngā ture ra,
He whakahoki mai i te waiora,
Hoki mai ai te mauri ki ahau ī.
Ko wai tērā e tū mai i Miti-mai?
Ko Te Whiti! Titia iho te raukura i a Te Āti Awa ē!

Te Whiti's house Miti-mai, on a slope overlooking the town, was built for him in European style by returned prisoners. Its full name was Miti-mai-te-arero.

SITTING IN MY HOUSE

Sitting in my house, I suddenly start up
As the clouds fly towards me, bringing longing
For the people thrown down to disaster.
Te Āti Awa, rise up and seek
The true path, the deeds done
By Te Whiti and his companions,
So the life-force will return to me!

The tables at Te Niho are spread, are spread.
Sir, convey your great laws to us!
What must we do to survive?
We must make our way to Parihaka
And Nohomairangi's house.
But Te Whiti is the man who has discovered those laws,
Bringing health to us once more
So the life-force returns to me.
Who is that standing by Miti-mai?
It is Te Whiti! Place your plumes on the heads of Te Āti Awa.

APPROACHING clouds are seen as bringing longing for the people who live in the direction from which the wind is blowing. These are Te Whiti's tribe of Te Āti Awa, whose land has been taken and who are still being persecuted by the Government. They are urged to continue their struggle and so give others the strength to continue also.

Te Niho, Te Whiti's well-appointed dining hall.

In this family group Nohomairangi, Te Whiti's son, is seated on the right. All wear the raukura.

In the second verse the poet speaks of the hospitality extended to all at Te Niho, Te Whiti's large dining hall. He, or she, speaks of the prophet's son Nohomairangi then ends by celebrating the role and teachings of Te Whiti, who has given his supporters new life and hope. Te Whiti is visualised as standing by his house, Miti-mai, and is asked to affirm the resolution and the mana of his people by placing in their hair the raukura, the white feather which is his emblem.

18
Lament for Parata

FOR 30 YEARS after the seizure of the Waikato lands, King Tāwhiao's determined search for justice and his prophetic sayings were a source of hope to his dispossessed people. Until 1881 he and his close followers lived with their Ngāti Maniapoto allies in Te Rohe Pōtae, the region that became known to the Pākehā as the King Country. After making peace with the Government in that year he was free to travel, and with his entourage he visited and wept over their wāhi tapu, the sacred places which had been taken from them. He led a deputation to England in the vain hope that Queen Victoria would restore their lands to them, and on his return he continued to seek ways in which Māori voices could be heard.

Shortly before his death in 1894, Tāwhiao bade his tribes farewell and announced his successor with these words:

> Papā te whatitiri, ka puta Uenuku, ka puta Matariki.
> Ko Māhuta te kīngi!
>
> The thunder crashes, Uenuku appears, Matariki appear.
> Māhuta is the king!

In this way he associated the kingship of his eldest son, Māhuta, with the mana and tapu of the thunder, the rainbow god Uenuku, and the constellation of Matariki (the Pleiades), which rose at dawn in the early winter to signal the start of a new year. His people treasured this saying, and they composed for Māhuta a song which quoted from it.

Tāwhiao (1825-1894), the second king of the Waikato-Maniapoto tribes.

KO MĀHUTA TE KĪNGI

Ko Māhuta te kīngi, hei kīngi hou,
Hei kīngi tuatoru mo te ao katoa.

Ko Te Paki o Matariki hei anahera,
Hei omaoma i waenganui i te iwi nui.

Ma mātou koe e hari atu. Haere,
E Māhuta, haere ki te ao katoa!

MĀHUTA IS THE KING

Māhuta is the king, a new king,
A third king for all the world.

Māhuta (c. 1855-1912), the third king.

Te Paki o Matariki are his angels,
To speed amongst our people.

We will carry you forth. Go,
Māhuta, go out to all the world!

THE SONG celebrates Māhuta's kingship (he is the third king, after Pōtatau and Tāwhiao), then the roles of his people. Te Paki o Matariki, The Fine Weather of Matariki, is an expression referring to the King's followers, more especially his senior men. They are seen here as angels, intermediaries who will act on his behalf. In the last lines the singers assert that they will make Māhuta's mana and his concerns known to the entire world.

James Cowan describes a performance he witnessed on an occasion when Māhuta was being welcomed by a Waikato community. First,

Māhuta's band marched on to the marae playing its tune, a modified version of 'an English popular air'. The song was sung by a group of men and women, then Māhuta walked slowly on to the marae and his people rose to their feet and bowed to him.

Soon after the song's composition it was incorporated in adapted form in a lament, described as a hīmene or hymn, which was composed by the son of a man named Parata.

KA HAERE A PARATA

Ka haere a Parata ra ki Te Paeroa
Kia kite i te hui nui mo te kīngi hou.
Ko Māhuta te kīngi, hei kīngi hou,
Hei kīngi tuatoru mo te ao katoa.
Ko ana mokopuna ra ko te anahera,
Hei omaoma i waenganui i te iwi nui.
Ka haere a Parata ra ki Hauraki,
E kore e hoki mai kia kite i te iwi nui.
Ma mātou koe e mihi atu. Haere,
E Parata, haere ki a Tāwhiao!

King Māhuta's flag bore his name in full, the seven stars of Matariki (the Pleiades), the rainbow, which is the sign of the god Uenuku, and other emblems. The Tainui canoe brought his tribal ancestors from the homeland of Hawaiki.

The expression Te Paki o Matariki, the Fine Weather of Matariki, referred to Māhuta's senior men. It was also the name of the official publication of the King Movement from 1891 to 1902. This issue carries a message from Māhuta.

PARATA SETS OUT

Parata sets out for Te Paeroa
To see the great meeting for the great king.
Māhuta is the king, a new king,
A third king for all the world.
His little ones are the angels,
To speed amongst our people.
Parata sets out for Hauraki
And will not come back to see our people.
We will send you our sad greetings. Go,
Parata, go to Tāwhiao!

PARATA MAY have lived somewhere near Matamata, for his wairua, his soul, will pass through Te Paeroa (or Paeroa) and the Hauraki region on its way northwards. Possibly there was a meeting at Paeroa at this time to welcome Māhuta, and Parata's wairua was thought to be making its way there to honour the King and be present a last time at a tribal meeting. As so often in waiata, the poet mourns a passing yet affirms that life will continue. In the underworld Parata will be received by Tāwhiao, who has gone before, and for those who remain in 'te ao mārama', the world of light, there will be Māhuta and the tribes that support him.

Notes

Introduction

For information about the music of waiata and other songs, see McLean and Orbell 1975. There are several other, less common, kinds of waiata besides those discussed here. The word 'waiata' cannot be translated. The term is now also used to refer to all melodic songs, including contemporary ones influenced by Western music.

The Pākehā missionary is Thomas Kendall (as published in Elder 1934:137).

1 Lament for a Rangatira

The text is from James Cowan (1930:108); there is no information as to locality or date, but it appears to be old. William Yate (1835:136) made the remark about the soul's being sung out of the body. Sometimes tangihanga lasted for longer than three days and nights, for they continued until the last of the parties of mourners had paid their respects.

Arapeta Awatere explained to the writer that the expression 'kahu tahu-whenua' refers to a cloak of red kākā feathers and 'kahu tahu-ā-rangi' to a cloak of (blue-black) tui feathers. For another waiata tangi which refers to a similar canoe voyage which may be both actual and mythical, see McLean and Orbell 1975:205. Sometimes in tradition the canoe for the dead is said to be under the captaincy of Whiro, while on other occasions it appears that the crew are ancestral spirits. Sometimes at a funeral the body was placed in a small canoe, and sometimes a small model of a canoe, with sail and paddles, was placed in a funerary monument or burial cave to provide a vessel for the wairua's voyage.

2 Te Ika-here-ngutu's Lament for His Children

The text is from Grey 1853:9, where it is entitled 'Ko te tangi a Te Ika-here-ngutu mo ana tamariki i mate taua etahi, i mate kongenge etahi', Te Ika-here-ngutu's lament for his children, some of whom died at the hands of a war party and others from disease. The word 'tamariki' can refer specifically to sons rather than children, and may do so here. Information has been taken from Ngata and Te Hurinui (1961:250-3) and Colenso (1881:65-6). Pomare and Cowan (1930-4:II, 73) say it was Te Āmio-whenua that caused the deaths in battle lamented by Te Ika-here-ngutu; for an account of Te Āmio-whenua, see Smith 1910:202-20. Sheffield (1963:40) says Tōtara-i-ahua, a rangatira of Ngāti Whātua, bought a musket, which he named Hūteretere, from a visiting ship before setting out with Te Āmio-whenua.

For the idea that both food and human beings disappear into Te Rēinga, see McLean and Orbell 1975:87. For an account of the tohi ceremony as performed on the West Coast, and quotations from karakia similar to that from which the poet quotes, see Taylor 1855:74-8. Grey's information about Te Wherowhero accompanies the text he publishes; Kati probably died in the 1840s. White's account (1874:218) occurs in a novel which he tells us is factually based; he lived among the Māori people in the Hokianga district from 1835 to 1850.

3 Love Song

The text is from Orbell MS 1977:II, 559-60, where there is a fuller discussion. The date of composition is not known; it was first published in 1905, but must be considerably older than this.

4 Te Rarawa's Protest

George Grey (1853:302) published this song without explanation, but among his papers in the Auckland Public Library (Grey MS 66: 609-10) there are a text, a translation and explanatory notes. The writer is indebted to the City Librarian for permission to use this manuscript.

A fuller discussion is in Orbell MS 1977:II, 316-9; for relations between co-wives, see Orbell MS 1977:I, 21-4. It is assumed from the reference to Taumata-whārangi that Te Rarawa lived near Waitara and belonged to Te Āti Awa.

5 The Song about Turner's House

The text is from Dieffenbach 1843:II, 312-3. For Wesleydale see Owens 1974 and Williment 1985; for Turner's return visit, Chambers 1982:61.

Evidence that this song was composed some time *after* the destruction of 'Turner's house' is provided by the name Hōhepa (which could only belong to a convert — yet Turner and his fellow missionaries had made no converts), and by the reference to two books of the Bible. Although instruction in reading and writing had been available at Wesleydale, no translations of biblical writings had been published at this time. Translations of short extracts from some books of the Bible, including Genesis and Matthew, were printed in August 1827, soon after the mission's destruction; but the poet is probably referring to the longer extracts from Genesis and Matthew which appeared with other writings in 1830, or to the translations of their entire texts which appeared in 1833.

The song was published in 1843. Probably it was composed in the early or mid-1830s, when Māori enthusiasm for Christianity was at its peak.

6   Lament for Tāmati Tara-hawaiki

This is one of a small group of songs concerned with Christianity which was collected by the Rev. Richard Taylor, one of the few Pākehā to show an interest in them. The text is in Taylor's papers in the Auckland City Library (Taylor MS 22, n.b. 8 [p.6]); for permission to use it, the writer is indebted to the City Librarian. A translation appears in a book by Taylor (1868:35), and it is said there that Tāmati (or Thomas) was one of the earliest Christian teachers of the Ngāpuhi people. Taylor probably heard the song on the West Coast where he was living, for his text has the letter *h* omitted in some places and this omission is in accord with some West Coast speech. In the present text the *h* has been restored.

For the conversion to Christianity, see Wright 1967 and Owens 1974.

7   Te Whare-pōuri's Lament for Nuku-pewapewa

The text and information about it are in Ngata 1959:152. For Nuku-pewapewa and Te Whare-pōuri, see Downes 1914-16, Downes 1912 and Best 1918:102-9.

Tariao is now sometimes said to be the morning star, the implication being that it is Venus (see for example King 1977:27), but traditionally this name was given to a star which shines in the early dawn before the appearance of Venus; Grace (1959:41) speaks of 'the stars of the morning, Tawera [Venus as the morning star] and Tariao', Cowan (1910:196-7, 263) speaks of Tariao as a twinkling star which is the harbinger of the morning star, and Williams says it is 'a star in the Milky Way'. So far, it has not proved possible to identify this star.

8 Lament for Te Iwi-ika

The text is from a manuscript written at Waikouaiti in 1894 or soon afterwards, preserved by F. R. Chapman, and now in the Hocken Library in the University of Otago (MS 416A, song no. 3); for permission to use it, the writer is indebted to the Librarian. The presence of the loan word 'rori', road, suggests that the song may have been composed in the 1840s or later, though it is possible that an old song was modified then to include this word.

In the second line the passage 'waniwani amu a wekuna' is of uncertain meaning, and the translation of the first three lines is accordingly tentative. In the South Island dialect the sound *k* is sometimes substituted for *ng*.

For the South Island story of Tāne see Wohlers 1974:8-10, 34-6 and, for Tāne's waters of life, Beattie 1939:35; some North Island versions are similar, but not identical. For Rangi-whakaūpoko-i-runga, Rangi-who-forms-the-head-above, see Beattie 1939:29. In the South Island, the house which stands in the underworld is sometimes called not Poutererangi but Whare o Pohutukawa, Pohutukawa's House (Beattie 1939:33); the North Island belief was that the souls made their way down the dangling roots of a pohutukawa tree, and in the South Island, where the pohutukawa does not grow, the name of this tree came to be regarded as the name of a person. In this song, Poutukutia appears to be another version of Pohutukawa.

9 Kāhoki's Song for Te Puku-atua

The text is from Grey 1853:118. Ngata (1959:186) gives a different version as one of a group of three songs which were apparently sometimes sung together. My reasons for preferring Grey's text are in Orbell MS 1977:II, 372-8. For a song by Kāhoki composed under different circumstances, see Ngata 1959:262. For loose translations, but no texts, of two other waiata aroha composed by her for Petera, see Cowan 1930:99-100; for further information about Petera, see Cowan 1910:211. For Angas's encounter with Kāhoki, see Angas 1847 (plate IX) and also Angas 1847a:I, 239.

10 Lament for Ngaro

The text and a translation are published by Davis (1855:177-8), who remarks that it 'was composed by Patuwhakairi, an aged Chieftainess of Hokianga, on the occasion of the death of her relative Ngaro, a young woman of great promise, and of considerable personal attractions'. Davis spent much of his childhood at Hokianga, and probably knew Ngaro.

In the second line the word 'torangi' is probably related to 'tō', 'set, of the sun'.

Although the last lines must refer to the prohibitions of the missionaries, it is not uncommon in waiata tangi for a poet to regret the circumstances of a person's funeral; compare lines 4–6 of a waiata tangi where the poet complains that persons who attended his daughter's tangihanga did not fire their muskets in her honour (McLean and Orbell 1975:274).

11   Mihi-ki-te-kapua's Song for Her Daughter

The first three verses of the text are from Ngata 1959:60–3, but the last one is a better version published by Mitchell (1972:61). The explanations come largely from Ngata; a rather different explanation is in Best 1925:457–8. Ngāti Ruapani are now for many purposes regarded as part of Tūhoe.

The first knowledge of writing was spread largely by Māori lay preachers who had studied at the mission stations then gone elsewhere to live and teach. Ihaka was a Christian, for his name is the Māori version of Isaac. The passage referring to Ihaka seems to imply that he would have read the letter aloud to Te Uruti.

For another version of the song Mihi has as her last verse, see Grey 1853:cvi. Some traditions give Matiu and Makaro as the names of the two islands which are known to the Pākehā as Somes and Ward Islands, and say they are daughters, or nieces, placed there by Kupe.

12   Tatai's Song for Te Toa-haere

The text, and much of the information, come from Ngata and Te Hurinui 1961:72–5; further information is in Cowan 1966:32–6. The meaning of the Arawa word 'mōuka' was explained to the writer by Arapeta Awatere.

Ngāti Pēhi are now known as Ngāti Whakauē, a hapū of Te Arawa. Mauao is also known as Maunganui and as the Mount.

13   Rangiamoa's Lament for Te Wano

The text and much of the information are from Ngata 1959:236–9; for the music, see McLean and Orbell 1975:114–8. For the Waikato War see Sinclair 1961 and Sorrenson 1963; for Rangiaowhia before the war, Cowan 1922.

The word 'wini' is formed from 'wind'. Many traditional expressions show the significance of the word 'toka' in such contexts as this. For the quotation in the last two lines, from a song by a South Taupō poet, see Pomare and Cowan 1930-34:I, 285-6.

The first verse is often sung on its own, and is sometimes attributed to Te Kooti Rikirangi.

14 The Exile's Lament

Elsdon Best (1925:I, 598) gives the text without a translation and explains that it was composed by Tawapiko as a lament for relatives deported to the Chathams. Best does not give Tawapiko's tribe; presumably he was from Tūranga. J. Kerry-Nicholls (1884:270-80) gives a translation, though not the text. In the last line Best has 'te mahi a raro', but Te Rangianiwaniwa Rakuraku informs the writer that the correct expression is 'te mahi a Rura'. Kerry-Nicholls' unpublished Māori text must have had this, for his translation has 'the deeds of Rura'.

Lyndsay Head explains that in Te Ua's teachings the name Rura is derived from the word 'ruler', and that Tama Rura, or 'Son Ruler', is Christ, who in the Book of Revelation is said to be coming at the millenium to rule the world. It is not certain, however, whether the people at Tūranga understood the name in this way.

For information about the wars, see Cowan 1922-3. Kerry-Nicholls quotes a man as saying that for a long time he expected Tāwhiao and Te Whiti to be taken up to the sky. Lyndsay Head informs the writer that around 1871-2, both Tāwhiao and Te Whiti had preached the imminence of the millenium.

15 Puhiwāhine's Song about Her Lovers

For the text of Puhiwāhine's song and the information given about her, the writer is indebted to Pei Te Hurinui Jones's valuable biography (1959-61). This is the only detailed study of the life and work of a nineteenth-century Māori poet.

16 Football Song

The text and explanations are from McLean and Orbell 1975:50-54, where a transcription of the melody is also to be found. The tune, like the words, is transitional in style.

Most of the terms used in rugby are loan words.

17 Song for Te Whiti

The text is recorded in an old manuscript book that belonged to the late Riki Ellison of Taumutu. Mr Ellison kindly allowed the writer to publish it (*Tu Tangata* 13, 1983). The book is among papers which Mr Ellison inherited from his great-grandfather H. K. Taiaroa, who grew up in Ōtakou (Otago); it belonged originally to Arehi T. Karetai of Waiari Kāinga, Ōtakou, for this name and address appear on the cover. On one page the date is recorded as 19 August 1894.

Te Niho (in full, Te Niho o Te Āti Awa), the dining hall mentioned in the song, was erected in 1889, so it seems that the song was composed in 1889 or the early 1890s.

18 Lament for Parata
James Cowan (1910:342-3) gives an account of Tāwhiao's proclamation and its incorporation in the song, and describes a performance. The text given here is from a manuscript in the Cowan papers in the Alexander Turnbull Library, Wellington (MS 39, item 8). For permission to use it, the writer is indebted to the Chief Librarian.

The lament for Parata is in McGregor 1903:59. The text given here is corrected from the manuscript of this book in the Auckland Public Library (NZMMSS 15:75); for permission to use it, the writer is indebted to the City Librarian. The manuscript is undated, but would seem from the surrounding material to have been written in the late 1890s.

The poets employ subtle patterns of repetition, and the translations given here do not do justice to them. In both songs the expression 'te iwi nui', referring to all the King Movement tribes, would have been translated as 'all the people' or 'all our people' if it were not that this would have left the translations with too many repetitions of the word 'all'. It has therefore been translated as 'our people'.

For another Waikato song in which a soul is sent to Tāwhiao in the next world, see McLean and Orbell 1975:205, where the relevant passage has been added to an ancient song.

Glossary

Most Māori words are unchanged in the plural. The macron indicates a long vowel.

haka	dance, dance song
hapū	tribe, or section of a tribe
kāinga	settlement, unfortified village
kūmara	sweet potato
mana	status, power
marae	ceremonial courtyard in front of a meeting-house or, formerly, the house of a rangatira
mauri	living essence or spirit of a place or person; object containing the spirit of a place
oriori	oriori, a kind of song addressed to a child
pā	fortified village, fortress
Pākehā	person of European descent
pātere	pātere, recited song composed in reply to insults
poi	light ball with string attached which is swung rhythmically by singers
rangatira	chief, man of rank and substance
raukura	plume worn on the head
tangihanga	funeral
taniwha	supernatural being living in the water or under the ground
tapu	sacred, sacredness, under supernaturally sanctioned restriction
tohunga	expert, generally a religious expert; priest
waiata	waiata, one kind of melodic song
waiata aroha	waiata expressing longing and love

waiata tangi	waiata expressing grief, lament
waiata whaiāipo	love song, woman's waiata addressed to a man or men she loves, or claims to love
wairua	soul, believed to leave the body during dreams and after death

References

Angas, G. F. 1847. *The New Zealanders Illustrated.* London.

—————— 1847a. *Savage Life and Scenes . . . .* London.

Beattie, J. H. 1939. *Tikau Talks.* Dunedin.

Best, E. 1918. 'The land of Tara and they who settled it.' Part IV, *Journal of the Polynesian Society* 99-114.

—————— 1972 (1st ed. 1925). *Tuhoe: Children of the Mist.* 2 vols. 2nd ed. Wellington.

Chambers, W. A. 1982. *Samuel Ironside in New Zealand 1839-1858.* Auckland.

Colenso, W. 1981. 'Contributions towards a better knowledge of the Maori race.' *Transactions and Proceedings of the New Zealand Institute* 13:57-84.

Cowan, J. 1910. *The Maoris of New Zealand.* Christchurch.

—————— 1922. *The Old Frontier.* Te Awamutu.

—————— 1922-23. *The New Zealand Wars.* 2 vols. Wellington.

—————— 1966 (1st ed. 1934). *Tales of the Maori Bush.* 2nd ed. Wellington.

Davis, C. O. B. 1855. *Maori Mementos . . . .* Auckland.

Dieffenbach, E. 1843. *Travels in New Zealand.* 2 vols. London.

Downes, T. W. 1912. 'Life of the Ngati Kahu-ngunu Chief Nuku-Pewapewa.' *Transactions and Proceedings of the New Zealand Institute* 45:364-75.

—————— 1914-16. 'History of Ngati-Kahu-ngunu.' *Journal of the Polynesian Society* 23-25 *passim* (7 chapters).

Grace, J. Te H. 1959. *Tuwharetoa.* Wellington.

Grey, G. 1853. *Ko Nga Moteatea . . . .* Wellington.

Jones, Pei Te H. 1959-61. 'Puhiwahine — Maori Poetess.' *Te Ao Hou* 28-34 (7 instalments).

Kerry-Nicholls, J. H. 1884. *The King Country . . . .* London.

King, M. 1977. *Te Puea: A Biography.* Auckland.

McGregor, J. 1903. *Popular Maori Songs: Supplement No. 2.* Auckland.

McLean, M. and Orbell, M. 1975 (revised ed. 1990). *Traditional Songs of the Maori.* Auckland.

Mitchell, J. H. 1972 (1st ed. 1944). *Takitimu.* 2nd ed. Wellington.
Ngata, A. T. 1959. *Nga Moteatea.* Vol. 1. Wellington.
Ngata, A. T. and Te Hurinui, P. 1961. *Nga Moteatea.* Vol. 2. Wellington.
Orbell, M. 1977. 'Themes and Images in Maori Love Poetry.' 2 vols. Thesis, University of Auckland.
Owens, J. M. R. 1974. *Prophets in the Wilderness: The Wesleyan Mission to New Zealand 1819-27.* Auckland.
Pomare, M. and Cowan, J. 1930-34. *Legends of the Maori.* 2 vols. Wellington.
Scott, D. 1975. *Ask That Mountain: The Story of Parihaka.* Auckland.
Sheffield, C. M. 1963. *Men Came Voyaging.* Christchurch.
Sinclair, K. 1961. *The Origins of the Maori Wars.* Wellington.
Smith, P. S. 1910. *Maori Wars of the Nineteenth Century.* 2nd ed. Christchurch.
Sorrenson, M. P. K. 1963. 'The Maori King Movement 1858-85.' In *Studies of a Small Democracy,* R. Chapman and K. Sinclair (eds). Auckland.
Taylor, R. 1855. *Te Ika a Maui* . . . . London.
─────────── 1868. *Past and Present of New Zealand.* London.
Te Hurinui, Pei. *See* Jones, Pei Te H.
White, J. 1874. *Te Rou, or the Maori at Home.* London.
Williams, H. W. 1971. *A Dictionary of the Maori Language.* 7th ed. Wellington.
Williment, T. M. I. 1985. *John Hobbs 1800-1883* . . . . Wellington.
Wohlers, J. F. H. 1874. 'The mythology and traditions of the Maori in New Zealand.' *Translations and Proceedings of the New Zealand Institute* 7:3-53.
Wright, H. M. 1967. *New Zealand, 1769-1840: Early Years of Western Contact.* Cambridge, Mass.
Yate, W. 1835. *An Account of New Zealand* . . . . London.

Credits

I am indebted to the directors of the following institutions for permission to reproduce photographs of works in their collections:

Alexander Turnbull Library: p.5, p.48 (Joseph Jenner Merrett, 1816–54, ink and grey wash, 164×253 mm), p.49 (Petera Te Puku-atua), p.63 (John Guise Mitford, watercolour, 1845), p.74 (Richard Laishley, 'Te Kooti at Rotorua 1887'), p.81 (Harding Collection), p.94, p.95.

Auckland City Art Gallery: p.41 ('Trevor Lloyd, 'Rangitoto', drypoint, 65×263 mm, presented by Connie and Olive Lloyd, 1973).

Auckland Institute and Museum: p.100.

Auckland Public Library: p.66, p.92, p.99, p.101.

Hawke's Bay Museum, Napier: p.72.

The Hocken Library, University of Otago: p.44, p.83 (Taonui and Major Keepa).

Methodist Church, Overseas Division, London: p.30 (both portraits).

National Library of Australia: p.14 (Joseph Jenner Merrett, 1816–54, 'War dance, New Zealand', watercolour, 192×303 mm, Rex Nan Kivell Collection NK1272), p.28 (J. Cochran, 'Revd. Nathaniel Turner', engraving, 113×92 mm, Rex Nan Kivell Collection NK1690).

The National Museum: p.49 (Rākapa Kāhoki), p.58, p.83 (Tōpine Te Mamaku, Rewi Maniopoto, Wahanui), p.93.

New Zealand Rugby Museum: p.88.

University of Canterbury Library: p.98.

For permission to take a photograph for publication, I am indebted to the Director of the Auckland Institute and Museum (p.62, photo Margaret Orbell). As well the following provided photographs: Ans Westra (p.4, p.57), Gordon Walters (p.15), Geoff Moon (p.53), Philip Temple (p.59), Lawrence Aberhart (p.89).

Lithographs and engravings in publications in the University of Canterbury Library were photographed by Duncan Shaw-Brown, Merilyn Hooper and Barbara Cottrell of the University's Audio-Visual Aids Department. The works are as follows:

G. F. Angas, *The New Zealanders Illustrated*, London 1847: cover, title page, pp.3, 9, 17, 21, 68.

E. J. Wakefield, *Illustrations to Adventure in New Zealand* . . . , London 1845 (Lithographs by Charles Heaphy): pp.25, 38.

W. Morley, *The History of Methodism in New Zealand,* Wellington 1900: p.29.

R. Taylor, *Te Ika a Maui* . . . , London 1855: p.32.

F. Hochstetter, *New Zealand* . . . , Stuttgart, 1867: p.33.

T. W. Downes, 'Life of the Ngati Kahu-ngunu Chief Nuku-Pewapewa.' *Transactions and Proceedings of the New Zealand Institute* 45, 1912: p.39.

E. R. Waite, *Scientific Results of the New Zealand Government Trawling Expedition, 1907* . . . , Wellington 1909: p.52.

J. Kerry-Nicholls, *The King Country* . . . , London 1884: p.75.

The photograph on p.78 is from the author's collection.